HORSE
LOVERS'
LIBRARY

BITS

Their History, Use & Misuse
plus Practical Advice on the Most
Effective Bits for Every Need

Louis Taylor

Photographs and Drawings
Rosemary Davison Taylor

Melvin Powers
WILSHIRE BOOK COMPANY
12015 Sherman Road
No. Hollywood, California 91605

FIRST EDITION

LIBRARY OF CONGRESS CATALOG NUMBER: 66-13928
DESIGNED BY THE ETHEREDGES

Published by arrangement with Harper & Row, Publishers, Inc.

ISBN 0-87980-231-6

CONTENTS

AN INTRODUCTION FOR YOUNG RIDERS— AND SOME NOT SO YOUNG

My great-uncle George was the best judge of horseflesh in the family. None of his seven brothers or their sons ever thought of buying a horse without having him inspect it. Only once did my father, a physician with a large practice, buy a horse without the help of Uncle George's opinion; and that cost him—but enough about judging horseflesh. What Uncle George taught me about bits is my concern here.

My grandfather had given me a Morgan mare for my tenth birthday. Though Uncle George knew the horses in the family better than he knew the people, my first long ride was a trip out to Uncle George's comfortable farm to show him my new mount.

Like most Morgans, my mare had lots of go in her. Any normal boy in those days knew as much about horses as one today

1

knows about cars. So I knew my mare had to be restrained. I knew better than to let her go faster than a jog on the hard pike (blacktop roads had not yet become common) or to let her become overheated. However, she fretted under my restraint; and the hair was wet on her neck and flanks by the time I turned off the pike and into the elm-lined drive that led to Uncle George's porticoed house and, farther on, to the spacious barn, cribs, and tool sheds.

As I turned in, and colts ran up to one fence bordering the drive, some horses in the barn lot nickered. Daisy, my mare, was delighted, for she was uncommonly gregarious. All the way down that long drive, at least the distance of a city block, she jigged and sidled, bobbing her head up and down. Twice she thrust her head into the bit so hard that I, hanging onto her for dear life, dusted the pommel of my saddle. As I passed the house, I caught sight of Uncle George sitting in his phaeton in front of the big tool shed. He was just sitting, watching me; and Fanny, a quiet and gentle old daughter of the Wilkes family, was standing patiently in the shafts.

His greeting, slight but adequate as were his movements with horses, was a little raising of his eyes and a softening of the straight line of his mouth. As Daisy and I fidgeted up to the phaeton, he took up his reins and turned Fanny a step to cramp the buggy so he could get out easily. Then he wrapped the reins around the whip, picked up his stockman's cane, eased himself out of the phaeton, and approached my dithering mare. Though his gait was arthritic, and standing upright was obviously a chore to him, the possibility of my jittery mare being a danger never entered my head. As she sidled past him, he put up his right hand and took hold of both my reins a few inches from the bit. Daisy's forefeet stopped. She gave a quarter turn on the forehand. Uncle George hooked his cane over his right arm. With his left hand he quietly stroked the now-dripping neck. The mare relaxed and made a movement as if to rub her lathered head on the old man's arm.

"Son, your mare's a little warm, ain't she?" was his first word to me.

"Yes, but she worked up all that sweat just coming in the drive. She had only started to turn a hair down by Hess's corner."

"Well, you better get down and walk her a little until she cools down."

As I dismounted, Dan, the chore boy six years my senior, obviously wanting an excuse to see my mare, came toward us from the cow shed saying, "Want me to put your mare away, Mr. Pegg?"

"No, we might need her; but you can lead this filly around until she simmers down if you want to. Take her in that pen over there so she'll know she ain't going any place and just walk her around."

He then turned to me. "Come, boy, let's sit down."

Holding my arm with one hand and using a cane with the other, he walked back to the phaeton and got in, motioning me to sit beside him.

"That's a good mare you have, but her kind is easy to spoil. Tom Duke broke her to harness for your grandfather, drove her a few months on his mail route, and then rode her a little to pay for her use. He's a good man with horses but not much of a saddle horse man. The mare is pretty green. Who told you to use that snaffle bit?"

"Dad. He said she'd never had a curb in her mouth."

"Your Pa's right, but if you keep on with that bit and hang onto it the way you were doing when you came down the drive, that mare will be a confirmed jigger and a puller to boot."

I was abashed and afraid to break the silence that followed his last statement. Finally I mustered courage to say, "Please, sir, would you tell me what bit to use and how to use it?"

"Well, that's a pretty big order, especially the last part. A man never quits finding out the answer to that, if he's a horseman. Even old Fanny here shows me a thing or two about what a bit is for now and then." With that, he gathered up his reins, backed the mare a few feet, turned the buggy around, and drove close to the pen where Dan was leading my now quiet mare in circles.

"When she dries off a little more, put a halter on her, let

her have a little water, take off her gear, and put her in that first stall," he instructed the boy.

Then he turned the mare onto the drive and headed for the pike, saying partly to himself, "Let's drive down the road a piece and figure a little."

The mare walked quietly. The singletree made a faint squeak in time with the mare's stride. As we turned onto the pike, Uncle George asked, "Son, why do you use a bit?"

"Why, because, er, uh—" I stammered, then blurted, "How else could you ride a horse?"

He chuckled and said, "I saw an Indian in Oklahoma Territory ride one without a stitch on either the horse or the rider. Guess maybe the Indian wore a breechclout, though."

I queried, "How did he stop the horse, or turn him?"

"Is that what you use a bit for?" was the surprisingly prompt rejoinder.

"Yes, I guess so—and some other things."

Good. Good for that 'other things.' But let's see about this stopping and turning business. How do you use a bit to stop a horse?"

"Why, pull on it, I guess," was my lame reply.

"Why does that stop him? He can pull harder than you can."

"I guess because if you pull hard enough the bit hurts him."

"And the hurt makes him stop?"

"I guess so."

"With some horses it makes them go faster. But, son, you've just said what men believed about the use of bits for thousands of years."

"What's that, Uncle George?"

"They thought a bit was useful because it caused pain and the way to make a horse do what you want is to hurt him in the right place at the right time."

"Well, I don't want to hurt horses."

"No, but you were giving your mare a little misery when she was coming down the drive a little while ago."

"But I couldn't let her run, not there!"

"No, and the only thing you knew to do was pull. Right?"

"I guess. What else could I do?"

"Well, you might have kept your hand lower than her head. That would have stopped pulling on the corners of her mouth, but until you and she learn what a bit is for, even that will not solve the problem, though until you learn a little more, a running martingale might help. That would put the pull on the bars of her mouth and help to keep her from fighting her head."

He turned Fanny into a gateway of a farm. High enough overhead to permit the passage of a large load of loose hay was a crosspiece joining the gateposts and bearing the words WALNUT GROVE STOCK FARM.

The farm road led us back some quarter of a mile beyond the buildings to a half-mile straightaway track at the edge of a meadow. A bay trotter was being worked in a jogging cart on it and turned to come near us as we approached the little track.

The driver saluted my uncle, "Good afternoon, Mr. Pegg. I'd almost made up my mind you were going to disappoint me. I sure want your opinion on him before I decide whether to send him to the track."

"This city fellow dropped in as I got in the rig and detained me, but I guess we haven't kept you working that colt too long. He looks fresh as a daisy," said Uncle George, turning to me with, "Son, you know Floyd Garret."

My respect for the driver of the trotter was such that I was somewhat embarrassed and hastily replied, "Oh, yes sir," and gave an awkward, "How do you do, Mr. Garret," to the young man in the jogging cart.

Uncle George got out of the phaeton and used hands as well as eyes to inspect the gelding, then said to Garret, "You've warmed him up enough to let him trot out a little. Take him up and down a few times."

I was all eyes, of course. The second time the three-year-old came past us he was hitting what must have been about a three-minute clip. The sound of those hoofs, the rippling of the muscles, and the flash of the feet sent shivers up my back. As Garret reached the end of the straightaway and turned to come back past us, Uncle George stepped out into the middle of the track.

He grasped his cane in both hands to steady himself and bent his knees, evidently to get his eyes as near as he could to the level of the legs coming toward him. I was afraid for a moment he would not get out of the way of the horse coming toward him with ever increasing speed. Just in time, he straightened up and walked to the side of the track nodding his head in approval. The cart reached the other end of the straightaway and turned. This time those driving hind legs swung so quickly into racing speed that the little cart was almost jerked off the ground, yet I could see no movement of hands on reins or any other signal given by the driver.

Uncle George motioned with his hand for Garret to stop. The gelding had started with what to me seemed terrific speed, and the driver seemed to be putting a good deal of pressure on the reins. I was amazed that he slowed the gelding down and brought him quietly to a stop in front of us without any apparent extra pull on the reins. I watched this closely because of Uncle George's recent question about what a bit was for.

"Floyd, I think he's a good one—action straight, and you've legged him up slowly and got him into good hard condition. He's ready for anything you ask of him," was my uncle's verdict.

"Thank you very much, Mr. Pegg, and thank you for coming over—you, too, Louis—I'll take him in tomorrow," Garret replied.

Fanny trotted out the Garret drive with a will and turned toward home on the pike so eagerly that Uncle George had to take a good hold on the reins to keep her from trotting too fast on the hard road.

"Well, boy, did you learn anything about what a bit is for?"

"I thought I did, but I don't know. Mr. Garret was holding that gelding pretty tight when he was trotting faster than most horses can gallop, but somehow he slowed him down without pulling as hard as you are to hold Fanny in. He seemed to be using a bit for something more than just pulling to slow down or turn."

The old gentleman beside me chuckled. "You did learn a good deal! A good horseman uses a bit to 'talk' with. A horse's brain is better at many things than yours is, but it isn't made for understanding language—not the way you do by listening to different combinations of words and understanding them. Any horse will soon learn certain words as signals, but that isn't enough language for a fine horseman. He knows that a horse understands movements and pressures—physical things. Men have used many devices to communicate with horses—a pair of sticks (they can tell a horse a limited number of things), a special kind of halter Westerners call a hackamore, even a knotted rope around his neck. But the most useful thing, horse-men agree, is a bit."

"Are you 'talking' to Fanny now?" I queried. "You seem to be just pulling a little harder than usual to make her slow down."

"Fanny and I don't talk the same 'language' as Floyd and his race horses, son. Fanny has learned my 'language' on the bit. If she hadn't, she'd be jittering the way your mare did when you came in the drive pulling lots harder than I am now—and Fanny is headed for home at feeding time and has more reason to be in a hurry than Daisy had."

"Sure, but she's older and gentler," I said.

After a reflective pause, Uncle George went on, "I believe you know a full brother of Fanny's that is not so gentle."

"What horse is that?" I asked, somewhat taken aback, for I thought I knew every good horse in the neighborhood and how he was bred.

"Bob McCreary's sorrel Joe."

"Oh, yes," I said, relieved that I was not totally ignorant. "He's so different from her I'd forgotten they were related. Mr. McCreary goes on some of the Riding Club rides, and Joe fusses and fumes going and coming. Mr. McCreary had blisters on his hands the last ride. I'd think he'd get a different bit."

The sage reply to my logic was, "Special bits can make up for bad hands sometimes, but Bob uses the best bit for him, a big bridoon with two reins and a running martingale. His hands on a severe bit in the mouth of a horse bred like Joe would make trouble. Either the man or the horse or both would be injured beyond repair."

"How come Fanny and Joe are so different, being full brother and sister, Uncle George?"

"Colts from the same sire and dam are often different, though from such uniform stock as ours they differ less than most. But the big difference between Fanny's actions and those of Bob's Joe is that Fanny has learned that a bit means something; to Joe it is a tug o' war."

"See here," he said as, holding one rein steady, he gave a quick extra pull on the other. The old mare ducked her nose, minced a few steps, and settled to a walk for at least ten steps as Uncle George relaxed rein pressure. As she took the next trot step, the signal on the reins was instantly given. The reins were as instantly relaxed, and she again settled to a walk.

"You see," he continued, "you don't just hang on and pull. You tell a horse something on the reins, if he has been taught what a bit means in your hands; and if he doesn't do what you want, you tell him again—and again and again if necessary. Floyd Garret and I don't use the same 'language' on a bit, but his horses know his, and my horses know mine. We use horses for different purposes. Did you notice anything special about the way Floyd's horse handled himself or the way he was bitted?"

"Yes," I replied. "He was reined pretty high by an overcheck. His head was very steady and his nose was out."

"What do you mean 'nose was out'?"

"It wasn't tucked in the way a good saddle horse's is. It wasn't even coming in the way a work horse's does when he's pulling hard and you use the reins to steady him. His head just seemed kind of stiff on his neck."

"Good!" exclaimed Uncle George. "At least you've learned that the bit on a work horse is for something more than stopping him, and you've caught the key to trotting speed."

I was pleased but puzzled and said, "Key?"

The answer was, "The key to all driving and riding is *balance*. A horse's head is his balancer. The 'language' of the hands and the kind of bit used determine what the head does."

Still puzzled, I asked, "But don't you breed special horses to trot or to be saddle horses or work horses?"

"Yes," was the answer, "that's the foundation; but to win races or stakes or pulling contests, the best of horses have to be balanced by hand and bit."

We had reached Uncle George's driveway. As we turned in, eight or ten yearlings and two-year-olds running in a pasture on our left galloped up to the fence to greet Fanny. She started to turn toward the colts.

As the old man restrained her by a quick deft move of one rein hand, he said, with a wave of his hand, "There! Look at them."

As we watched, the colts playfully competed for the spot closest to the fence and Fanny. They took nips at each other and a few kicks. Some galloped off a little way and circled back, coming up to the others with forefeet in air and striking.

"See that chestnut with a star," said Uncle George, pointing with his cane. "He's by a son of Highland Denmark and out of a Highlander mare. What do you see in his 'balancer'?"

I watched and considered carefully before answering. "Well, it's a beautiful head."

"Yes, it has to be, with his breeding; but how does he handle it?" the old man queried.

"He—he—" I fumbled and finally managed, "His neck is so long and flexible. Mostly he carries it up and arched so his head is almost straight above his shoulders; but when he bites, it shoots out almost like a snake when it strikes. His neck is so much more flexible than the others."

"That's right, boy, and he'll be ridden finally with a full bridle and the light hand on the curb will help out his natural balance."

At that moment, a sorrel yearling darted out from the little bunch, ran with incredible speed for a few rods, circled and dashed back.

"What about that Thoroughbred's 'balancer'?" demanded my teacher.

"He carries it poked out in front of him," I replied.

"What bit will help him use it to become the best hunter in this county?" was the next question in the catechism.

"I suppose a snaffle."

"You suppose right—one of those large Irish bridoons and light and very quiet and steady hands."

The colts had settled down and started to graze.

"Keep your eye on that bay filly," said my uncle as he gathered up the reins and started the old mare into a smart trot only to stop her in a few rods.

The colts, of course, all immediately broke into a gallop to race beside us—all except the bay filly. She trotted.

As he stopped Fanny, my questioner continued with, "What about her 'balancer'?"

"Well, sir, it was held high but forward because there is no arch in her neck—"

"And never will be," cut in my uncle. "The overcheck will prevent it; and that granddaughter of Joe Wilkes ought to do a mile in two minutes some day."

"Is that big black by Jehova?" I asked admiringly as an enormous two-year-old Percheron pushed his way to the fence.

"Yes," was the answer, followed by, "What is that arch in his neck for?"

I replied "I don't know. I can't see how that will help him pull."

"You don't use your eyes too well sometimes, boy. What does Charlie Miller do when he starts that team of gray mares on a heavy pull?"

"I guess I don't know, but once when he let me drive them to pull up the hay in the big barn and he'd stuck the fork pretty deep for a big load he yelled at me, 'Take hold of them lines, boy!' Maybe you mean he pulls on the lines."

"You're about right," said Uncle George. "For a good pull, a driver gets the 'balancer' in—settles his team on their haunches so they can push into the collars. He usually has pretty strong arms, so we use big snaffles or bar bits."

"Oh, yes," I broke in, hoping to prove I *could* use my eyes. "That's why you use a leather bit on old Dick. Charlie said he's an honest puller but tender in the mouth."

We left the colts to their grazing and play and drove into

the carriage shed. Uncle George told me to go get Dan to put the mare away. This hurt my pride a little, and I insisted I could do it. Uncle George chuckled and agreed.

As I hung up the harness I saw a running martingale hanging on a nail in a corner of the harness room. Unlike the other gear there, neatly arranged on wooden pegs, it had not been kept soft and clean by repeated soapings; but it was stout and the stitching was all intact.

I took the martingale from the nail, shook the dust off it, and went in search of Uncle George. I found him inspecting a raw place on the shoulder of one of the work horses and talking to Charlie Miller, one of the oldest and best hands on the farm.

"It must be that new collar," my uncle was saying. "Or maybe the hames aren't set right on it. The draft is too low and out too near the point of the shoulder." Then seeing me, "Got the mare put away, son? Where'd you find that old hunting gear?"

"I found it in the harness room, sir, and wondered if you'd mind my using it to see if it would help steady Daisy's head."

"Help yourself," he replied as he turned again to the problem of the sore shoulder.

I saddled and bridled my mare, putting my reins through the rings of the newly acquired martingale. With my rein loosely over my arm, I turned my back on Daisy while I closed the barn door. She put her head down to nibble at a tiny clump of grass growing in the protection of the stone foundation of the building.

I turned and pulled the reins to raise her head from the ground. The rings of the martingale had slid down. One of them caught over the buckle of one rein. When the mare tried to raise her head, the buckle held the martingale ring fast. In vain, Daisy tried to raise her head. She reared and struck. She shook her head violently and with one mighty tug upward broke the cheek strap of the bridle. The bit tore through her mouth. As she thrust her head on high, the bridle ripped off, breaking the throatlatch. It fell to the ground as Daisy dashed off down the long drive toward the public road. I was stunned, but not too stunned to be filled with visions of all the terrible things that might befall my beautiful mare on the highway.

Fortunately, I knew enough about horses not to run after her. As she careened down the drive, the colts in the pasture ran up to the fence delighted. Daisy checked and pranced over to the fence to smell noses. Charlie Miller had heard the running hoofs on the drive, looked out, and immediately taken proper action. He took the barnyard fence with considerable speed for a man of middle age, circled quickly and quietly around behind the colts, and got between Daisy and the open road.

Uncle George, holding a halter in his hand, was waiting for us—Charlie, Daisy, and me—at the stable door. Charlie had made a sort of hackamore of what was left of the broken rein which I had quietly slipped around Daisy's neck while she was conversing with the colts across the fence.

"That's a pretty fancy halter Charles has made," chuckled the old gentleman, "But you'd better put this one on your mare and then come into the house. I have a little something for your birthday, too, though it's a little late; and it may be very useful for your trip home."

By the time I had tied my mare in an empty stall with her new halter and entered the big front room of the house, Uncle George was seated at his roll-top desk in the "alcove" that served him as an office. He pulled out the big bottom drawer and poked his cane under some loose folders revealing a package tied with harness-maker's thread.

"There," he said. "Pull out that package and open it. You'll have to cut the string. Here's a knife. Be careful not to cut through the paper."

What I found was two bits, a curb and snaffle, and a bundle of straps of beautiful English leather lightly tallowed.

"Do you know what that is, boy?"

"A bridle, I think, sir, and a beautiful one!"

"Yes, a full bridle of good English stock. It's been in that drawer for some years. I'll never have any more use for such gear, and it looks like you have urgent need. It's yours if you can put it together."

Under Uncle George's close scrutiny I eagerly set to work. I picked out the parts for the curb headstall—crownpiece with throatlatch, browband, cheekpieces (which gave me a little trouble until I discovered that two of the three cheekpieces in the bundle were identical and determined that the odd one must be for the snaffle headstall), chin strap, and lip strap. All went well until I got to the chin strap.

"No, son, not that way. Always remember that everything buckles from the left side of your horse and the end of each strap must point either down or back. That means that the tongue of every buckle must point either up or forward. The buckle end of each strap must come *from* the right side or *from* the bottom. Look at the cheek straps. You got them right. And the noseband. It's right; the buckle end comes under the jaw *from* the right, so the tab end of the noseband points to the rear.

"Start your curb strap from the other side of the bit; so when you buckle it, the tab end points to the rear, not toward the front of the horse's nose."

The lip strap completely stopped me. Uncle George came to my rescue with some amusement.

"You're right. There's no way you can put it on and have the tab end of the long strap pointing to the rear. That's the exception that proves the rule. Just attach the long strap on the right side. That'll make the buckle come on the left, and nobody has yet found a way to make a lip strap tab point to the rear!"

I managed to get the short snaffle cheek on the left side, but I put the long strap over the head on top of the curb crownpiece.

"No, son," I was corrected. " your snaffle bit lies on top of your curb and *inside.* That long strap goes under the main crown, but the cheeks of the snaffle are outside the noseband when the bridle is on the horse. And before we put it on, we'll remove that chin strap that you worked so hard to get right; and we'll replace it with a chain. Chains don't stretch and pinch the corners of a mouth the way straps do."

It pleased my uncle to see that I got the wide rein on the snaffle bit, with the buckle on the left.

"Do you know why the ends of the curb reins are stitched and the snaffle ones are buckled?" he asked. And then, as I started to buckle the ends, he stopped me with, "No, no, don't buckle them. That's just the point. We want to put guards on that rein and put it through martingale rings—yes, we have another martingale, better than the one you and Daisy finished. You see, no good horseman uses the curb reins through a martingale, but once in a long time there is a need to run the snaffle reins through a martingale, and this is one of those times. Your mare is used to a snaffle but not to a curb. So, you'll use the snaffle with martingale for several days before you begin to touch the curb. But you'll put rein guards on, so you will not get the martingale rings hung on the buckles again, though with these buckles there's less danger of that than with those monstrosities you had on your old reins."

From another drawer in his desk he extracted a pair of round leather disks. Each was slotted to allow a rein to pass through it.

"You'll have to work these a little in your hands," I was told. "They're pretty stiff. We may even have to whittle the slots a little to get the reins through, but we'll have to be careful not to make 'em too loose."

I did have some difficulty getting the reins through the slots of the guards. We had to whittle the one for the left rein, the one with the dainty buckle.

Uncle George himself put the new bridle on Daisy, telling me to watch closely how the snaffle fit snugly up into the corners of the mouth, riding on top of the curb. The chain, which replaced the chin strap, was adjusted so that the shanks of the curb bit could come back, when pulled, to a 45-degree angle with the mouth but no farther. The noseband and throatlatch were quite loose, so loose that I asked a question.

"Is the noseband supposed to be that loose?"

"That depends," was the reply. "On this mare, comfort is the main thing. We want her to be able to mouth those bits freely. The noseband must be loose enough for her to move her jaws in comfort. See that throatlatch?"

"Yes," I answered. "It's pretty loose, too."

"Not any too loose," was the response. "See if you can put your fist under it."

There was plenty of room for my fist.

"There won't be," said my teacher, "when she tucks her chin in. Many horsemen buckle a throatlatch snug and then wonder why their horses make a noise when they breathe!"

He continued with, "Now about nosebands. Some trainers buckle them tight so a horse can't open his mouth. If he opens his mouth when the bit is pulled, they say he 'cheats on the bit.' Generally, I like a noseband plenty loose—for all purposes."

He put the snaffle reins through the martingale rings and then buckled them.

"Now take that martingale up so the rings can come up almost as high as your mare's withers but no higher."

This done, he asked me to mount.

"Now just take up your snaffle rein lightly," he said.

Daisy, of course, immediately started to move; but a knowing old hand on her noseband restrained her. With a thumbnail Uncle George made a light mark on the snaffle rein directly above the front of Daisy's chest.

"Now get off and slide that left rein guard back to within a few inches of that mark I made. Then make the right one just like it."

Both rein guards were right behind the bits, and he cautioned me to hold the bit firmly so that the mare's mouth would not be pulled as I slid the guards back.

"There," he commented when my task was completed. "Now that martingale will operate where it should, and your mare will not get a martingale ring caught on a buckle if she lowers her head. Better get along home, boy, the shadows are getting long. It'll be dark before you get home, and your pa will be wondering about you. Remember, keep that curb rein slack for several days. Then just start using it to politely ask her to tuck her chin for two seconds once in a while until she begins to get the idea of what it's for."

Seldom has life seemed better than on that ride home. The mare was relaxed and responsive. The faint aroma of a healthy horse mingled with light perfume of new English leather. The meadow larks were making a final comment on the day, which was closing in a glorious sunset. What a birthday I had had. Not until years later did I realize that the best present of all had been Uncle George's gift of rare insight into real horsemanship.

1. BITS—AND
HOW THEY BEGAN

The sensible way to start a history, or at least the way we expect a history to start, is to begin at the beginning. This makes a history of bits and their use very difficult. Any history, someone of importance once said, is a pack of lies agreed upon. The trouble with a history of bits is that there isn't much agreement about the beginning. Aldous Huxley said, "In the raw, existence is always one damned thing after another, and each of the damned things is simultaneously Thurber and Michelangelo, simultaneously Mickey Spillane and Maxwell and Thomas á Kempis." He also said, "Closest to reality are always the fictions that are supposed to be the least true."

In the hope of making comprehensible the frequently simultaneous historical details I have gathered for this book, I shall give first an arbitrary and somewhat stylized summary of the early development of bits and their accessories.

EARLY MOUTHPIECES, SIDECLAWS, AND NOSEBANDS

There is a strong probability that the first horse that humans ever used for anything but food was a cripple or an animal emaciated by accident or illness. Such an animal could be controlled by goad or club. He needed nothing to restrain him. As horsemen grew bolder, they probably next used something resembling a halter. There is some evidence to indicate that the first bits, at least the first in the steppe country, consisted of sidepieces held together by a thong that went through the mouth. Then simple stiff mouthpieces were invented.

As horsemen grew bolder and used less emaciated horses, they began to invent bits that would control the horse by causing pain. In some parts of the world, the first invention was the joint of the mouthpiece, as we have it in our modern snaffle. Each of the two parts of this jointed mouthpiece, sometimes called the cannons, ended at its outer extremity in a cheekpiece provided with claws or spikes that dug into the side (the outside) of the horse's mouth when the reins were pulled. In other parts of the world, spiked nosebands were used. Sometimes they were used without bits. Sometimes the nosebands were used attached to the bits. Almost invariably they were hung low, much lower than we hang a modern bosal or hackamore (a properly used hackamore is hung just above the soft cartilage of the nose—as explained at length in my *Out of the West*). As those early bits, like all snaffles, would pull up toward the horse's ears whenever he threw up his head and stuck out his nose—as he does naturally in response to pain in his mouth—some horsemen used only the lower half of a studded or spiked noseband. It is obvious that if the cheekpieces (rings in a modern snaffle) are connected by a spiked strap under the jaw, the spikes will dig in whenever the horse thrusts his nose forward and upward and the bit is pulled toward the horse's ears. Even today we can see on tracks and in fields some horses ridden with a snaffle with their noses out and the bit pulling up on the corners of the mouth, toward the ears instead of on the bars of the mouth.

How long it took the ancients to discover the folly of this practice cannot be definitely established, but they did learn to use a sort of martingale (reins through rings held down by attachment to chariot or harness). With the martingale, horsemen were able to use a great variety of painful mouthpieces—disks, spikes, chains, etc. One of the classes of these hellish devices was called "The Echini" by Xenophon.

Modern scholars, some of them horsemen but experienced only in English or European horsemanship, are often somewhat perplexed by the use of those severe bits. Of course horsemen acquainted with the old Baja California jaquima and spade, those about whom Tom Lea has written in *The Hands of Cantu,* would understand. Probably the use of the slack rein of old western horsemanship could be traced to Xenophon. Certainly the English horsemanship, which includes keeping some pressure on reins at all times, comes down to us from the North. We might trace it to the Gauls, who probably brought to Greece the heavier (and heavier-headed) horses and the first curb bits.

Even in ancient Egypt there was some refinement of horsemanship that may give a clue to the origin of jacquima (hackamore) horsemanship. Those opulent valley dwellers used sidepieces that were essentially very long bars, though they were so highly (and sometimes symbolically) decorated that they could hardly be called "bars." The cannons of the bit were attached to the center of each bar, like some of our old-fashioned snaffles. The bars were kept at right angle to the horse's mouth by three cheek straps. A cheek strap was fastened to each end of the bar, and one to its center. The reins were fastened where the cannon joined the sidepiece. When the reins were pulled, the bars were pressed against the jaw. It is intriguing to note that this comes close to being an example of the use of the lever as we see it in the modern Pelham, or curb; and yet it was not until centuries later that the curb bit (I mean here the one involving the action of the fulcrum by use of chin chain or strap) was invented.

Cerveteri: detail of painting on Corinthian Column-Krater showing wedding procession (570-560 B.C.). Note branches of cheek piece of bridle used to keep side piece of bit at right angle to mouth. Detail from *The Birth of Western Civilization,* Thames and Hudson, London and M. Grant, McGraw-Hill Book Company

THE PSALION

In all the literature arising from scholarly research there are no clues to the origin of the *rozadera* (the part of the jaquima that comes in contact with the jaws when reins are pulled). The use of the *rozadera* to get flexion at the poll, and the balance and movements desired, is the key to the horsemanship of old Mexico and California that reached a refinement seldom if ever equaled by any other kind of horsemanship. One of the few clues to a possible source of the *rozadera* was the *psalion,* which is said to be a device used in conjunction with the bit. It is also suggestive of the modern hackamore bit, which is a bit only in name. The *psalion* consisted of two U-shaped metal straps. One of them went around the nose, the other under the jaw. The nose strap was placed some six inches lower than the jaw strap. The open ends of the U of the nose strap turned upward at right angles and were extended far enough to be attached to the open ends of the jaw strap. Reins were attached to the lower U, the one over the nose. Used in conjunction with a bit, this contraption acted much as does the type of modern hackamore bit that is provided with a removable mouthpiece. Pressure on the reins would cause pressure on the nose, on the jaw, and on the bit. As far as I can determine, this piece of hardware originated in the seventh century B.C. and continued to be used for many cen-

The ninth century B.C. Assyrian chariot horse's triple cheekpiece bridle holds side piece of bit at proper angle, as discussed in the text. From *Ancient Greek Horsemanship,* J. K. Anderson, University of California Press.

turies. It has been found in many diggings of the period of the Roman Empire.

It would be very logical and orderly if we could say that these double-U contraptions were followed in the historical development of the bit by the use of the mouthpiece as a fulcrum, thus creating the curb, with its chain under the jaw and its longer lever, the shank, attached to the reins. But as has been said, history is not logical. There seems to have been quite a lapse in time between the use of the metal U straps and the use of the curb with its leverage and fulcrum principle. Furthermore, the latter seems to have originated in a part of the world far removed from the region in which the former was used.

SUMMARY OF EARLY BITS

Many factors becloud the facts of the historical development of bits—types of horses used, conditions in which horses were kept, purposes for which horses were used, and the terrain over which they habitually traveled. In battles and even in sporadic forays, bits of the most primitive sorts and those of the most highly developed varieties were used simultaneously in the same area. However, for the sake of clarity, it may be useful to keep in mind, while studying the historical details I shall give presently, an "as if" or hypothetical outline of bit development.

The first artifacts that may readily be called bits consisted of little more than sidepieces connected by thongs or other perishable material. Next came the metal mouthpieces, sometimes jointed or formed like chain, then the claws that dug into the outsides of the mouth. Almost at the same time, the spiked or studded nosebands were used, sometimes in conjunction with the jointed bits. Next came the bits that had sidepieces joined by a metal strap under the jaw (sometimes called curbs, though they did not employ the leverage principle we associate with the word *curb*). While all these types were evolving, there were many variations or improvisations such as the long sidepieces held in place by triple cheekpieces so they would pinch the jaws on the outside. There were also the bits that foreshadowed the hackamore bit, the ones with the U-shaped band over the lower nose and the U-shaped band a little higher going under the jaw. Then came the bits with the hedgehog, the spiked or studded mouthpiece. Such were bits for literally thousands of years; and they seem not to have led into the development of the leverage curb and, subsequently, into the use of the leverage curb in conjunction with the snaffle or "straight" bit—the use of two bits and two reins or one bit and two reins, one employing leverage and the other using direct pull on the bars of the mouth.

Let us now leave this vantage point of the hypothetical and general, taken for convenience and clarity's sake, and try to get a closer look at the earliest bits and their use. To do so, let us go to what is generally regarded as the birthplace of civilization.

Among the several respectable guesses about when and where man first started to control man and, shortly, to control the horse, one of the easiest to believe is that it was somewhere not far from Mesopotamia and sometime prior to 4000 B.C. Just

Horse bit from Southern Russia, about eighth century B.C. *Horizon*, Spring, 1965

so, it is easiest for us to believe that the use of horses and the bits that made them most useful arose somewhere near what we now refer to as Mesopotamia. It is easiest to talk about the beginning of the use of bits if we assume this to be true, because more primitive bits have been dug up and more pictures of them in use have been unearthed in the general area of Mesopotamia, Egypt, and Greece than in all of the rest of the world. Also, our ancestors who lived in that vacationlike climate seem to have learned their ABC's earlier than did their neighbors. Because of that, we have earlier and more numerous written records of their use of horses and bits than we do of their neighbors.

Though the assumption that the Tigris-Euphrates Valley was the origin of civilization and chief source of horsemanship (and the bits that are such an important part of horsemanship) would make easy the study of the history of bits, considerable evidence has been dug up, much of it very recently, to make the student's task much more complicated. Diggings in 1954 revealed some surprising evidence about European horsemen to the north. In 1956 startling discoveries of rock paintings in the Sahara revealed horsemanship and the use of bits in that country when the climate was very different from what we associate with the Sahara, so different that human life in communities flourished in the land that is now, in the words of the discoverer, M. Henri Lhote, "cursed with an inhuman climate." These are but two of a number of recent discoveries that force even the most casual student to suspect that, parallel with the development of bits and other important human achievements in Mesopotamia and Egypt, there were similar if not even more advanced equestrian developments elsewhere in the world.

FOREIGN INFLUENCES

The Mesopotamians had neighbors to the north who roamed the vast grass lands (cluttered with a couple of mountain ranges) that stretched from the Volga almost to the Danube. They did not go in much for book learning (in fact they did not even have an alphabet), but they left some evidence that they were better horsemen than the southerners. These Sarmatians, Parthians, and the later Scythians, as we call them, were more or less the grandparents of the Tartars, whose horsemanship is so spectacular that even Hollywood makes capital of it now and then.

Then there were people who the archaeologists tell us seemed to take their styles of acting and manufacturing from a little village called La Tène, located in Switzerland near what was to be, centuries later, the birthplace of Neufchâtel cheese. These people are called variously Celts, Gauls, and Gaels. They were mentioned in the first Latin book schoolboys used to read. They left "sign," as big game hunters might say, from the North Sea to Greece and from the country of the Sarmatians to the west coast of Ireland. They, too, seemed to be better horsemen than scribes. Some of their bits dug up in Bavaria in 1954 look so much like the bits of Grecian charioteers that we are left wondering if the men of Athens did not copy their driving bits from the riding bits of the Gaels (or Celts, if you prefer). All we can learn supports the belief that men of the North, and especially men living in mountainous country, rode some time before their southern neighbors in less rugged terrain ventured out of their chariots and onto their horses' backs—unless of course in battle the sound for retreat made them cut the traces, jump on the backs of whatever chariot horses were still on four legs, and hightail it for home.

The parallel developments of bits and their use—by the Celts, the Sarmatians, and Scythians of the steppes, the dwellers in the Sahara, and probably some others—were diffused long before the dawn of history. In spite of the absence of air transport, man got about. "Give a man a horse he can ride" and he will soon find (if he is capable of riding well) that it is much pleasanter to sit a horse than to grub for food in the earth or do other tedious work to fill his belly and put clothes on his back. The have-nots found that the use of the bit and a horse to wear it enabled them to take from the haves. This they did, from Ireland to Mongolia and from the North Sea to the Mediterranean.

We might almost say that the bit was the father of rugged individualism. Roaming and predatory riders of horses were attracted to the riches of the highly civilized Tigris-Euphrates Valley like bees to an orange grove in bloom. Some of them left behind bits, objects more valuable than what they stole—at least more valuable to the Sumerians, Babylonians, and Egyptians. Evidently the marauders were so clever, or they were so few, or, perhaps, their thieving was so swift, that they left no horses in ancient Sumer—at least the Sumerians used bits only on donkeys. However, the mysterious Hyksos occupied the land of Babylon for a brief while and from them the valley dwellers learned to use the horse, though they used him chiefly to draw chariots—suitable to their terrain though impractical for nomads roaming rougher lands.

Whether or not we credit Mesopotamia with the invention and development of the bit, a study of its history in that land gives us excellent clues to its use in all other parts of the world; for the nomadic bit-users and inventors raided each other, and practically all of them at one time or another—Scythians, Gaels, Numidians, Semites, and others—raided the fertile valley of the Tigris-Euphrates. In so doing, they left evidence of their uses of the bit and, in most instances, samples of bits that are only now coming to the light of day.

2. THE ROLE OF THE BIT

From the time when man first stood upright and learned to swing a club at his neighbor (and Adam and Eve raised Cain), until today, when he can traverse interstellar space and, if he will, blow himself and all other life off the earth, his progress has not been steady. Rather, it has been a series of lurches and leaps. Usually some invention, discovery, or unusual insight has been the springboard for each of these lurches or leaps—the invention (or discovery) of the use of fire, the invention of the wheel, or, more recently, the discovery that ours is a world of processes and four dimensions.

One of the most important of these springboards was the discovery of the use of the horse. In various parts of the world, man first used the horse for food, ate his flesh, drank his blood and used his hide for clothing, then tied him to burdens to be dragged. (Only the Scythians and their kinsfolk rode the horse before man used him in chariots.) However, it was the invention of the bit that made the horse the great tool of man. First the man with the chariots, then the man on horseback brought order out of chaos (or made big groups out of little ones) by subjugating his neighbors and enslaving his enemies and foreigners. From the time of Sumerian chariots, sixty centuries ago, until the coming of the railroad, the horse was man's land transportation (with a little help from the camel in exotic places). Not only was the bit a necessity in making the horse play the important role in practical affairs of government, warfare, and transport; it also was essential in making the horse play a leading part in the refinements of courtly life when civilization developed to the point of sprouting frills. In sport, man used the horse to play polo long before the first Greek threw a discus. The Oriental polo player's bits were as different from ours as were his crescent-shaped mallets, but his bits were just as vital to the sport as ours, even though he was not trying to use race horses in a sport that requires quick stops and extreme collection.

The change in the horse's role in the Christian world attests the mercy of the Christian God. No longer does the horse play a major role in tilling the fields, providing transportation, or (most merciful of all) in serving men in their mass slaughter of each other. However, more horses are being used by men in the United States today than ever before, and according to a recent study, the annual expenditure by horsemen just to be horsemen is in the billions of dollars. Not the smallest part of this expense is for bits, and bit styles are changing more rapidly than the styles of milady's hats. The horse has graduated from beast of burden to playmate and article of conspicuous consumption. For these roles his bits must be not only useful but also ornamental and fashionable.

3. THE HORSE'S SUITABILITY FOR THE BIT

With great respect (and sorrow) for the ass and his unnatural offspring, for the cow, the camel, and the elephant, I am sure the horse has shared in more of human life than any other animal except the dog. Reasons for this fact are numerous, but most prominent among them is the ability of the horse to wear and respond to the bit in a unique way.

A properly trained horse so co-ordinates his body balance with variations of pressure and rhythm on the bit that his center of balance (in his natural and free state it is most of the time at a point just behind his shoulders) shifts from forehand to haunches instantaneously in response to a light hand on the bit. When his neck flexes at the poll, his hocks come forward under his body. If the flexion is extreme and his head is raised, by a light hand, his forehand will leave the ground. If he is taken on the snaffle properly, his nose goes forward, his hocks move to the rear, and he carries most of his weight on his forehand. If proper pressure is put on the bit, if the direction of the pull on the reins is correct and the proper amount of impulsion is supplied by leg or heel aid, the center of balance will move slightly to the rear, the stride will shorten, and the height of action will increase to the limit of the horse's ability—his natural ability without crippling gimmicks. If any other animal can be taught to respond to a bit in any one of these ways, he will be a miraculous wonder and a good attraction for a circus side show. Yet any good trainer can teach any reasonably well-bred horse to respond in all of them.

Other animals, it is true, have lower jaws provided with a toothless space of gums on which a bit can rest when the mouth is closed. I have seen oxen with bits in their mouths and have ridden on roundups beside mules that were as handy at outthinking a cow as any horse alive. I have ridden a few good saddle mules—enough to get the feel of their mouths. Of this I am sure, though of much concerning the mystery of what a bit means to a horse I confess total ignorance: No other animal can be easily taught to coordinate his whole body balance, speed, and rhythm with bit pressure. No other animal can readily be taught to flex at the point just behind the head, to mouth a bit lightly and *communicate to his rider* (though precious few riders even today have sense and sensitivity enough to get the message!) : Yes, some good saddle mules rein well and stop well. At some jobs requiring a good rein and a good stop, an exceptional mule under an exceptional rider can outdo most horses, but the lightning response to the light rein belongs to the horse alone. The ox and the ass can be turned to this side or that by a lateral pull on the rein. They can be brought to a stop by a pull on both reins. Only the horse can readily be taught by a skilled horseman "to perform," in the words of Tom Lea, "that mode of advancing *levade* with ironshod feet pawing air, to the terror of Indian afoot." *Levade* is that show ring movement in which a horse rises and balances on deeply bent haunches with forelegs drawn up.

"Such a horse," said Xenophon over twenty-two centuries ago when referring to a horse executing this maneuver (without the shod hooves), "will be able to gather his hind legs well under his fore."

Without a bit or some substitute, such as a tack collar or jaquima, no rider can put his horse through such a performance. Even with a bit, no ox, ass, or mule can be persuaded to perform it. It is the horse's unique structural suitability for and response to the bit that make it possible for him to perform in many unique ways in harness as well as under saddle.

Artificially high action, in harness and under saddle, has long been an important adjunct to man's pageantry and other frills of civilization. It is vital to the horse in his long-time role as an article of conspicuous consumption—a must for the horse destined for the carriage trade. Various gimmicks have been devised to increase a horse's action—feet of crippling length, heavy shoes, working the horse in training with chains around his feet until the feet become sore and painful to use (see discussion of this practice among Walking Horse trainers in an article entitled "The Torture Must End" in *Sports Illustrated* early in 1960). Some trainers apply a caustic to the legs just before entering the show ring—a trick I have seen backfire so badly that the animal became unmanageable and had to be taken from the ring. But all such gruesome gimmicks are futile without the bit, the proper bit properly used.

Only the horse, because of his peculiar adaptability to the bit, can be induced to travel with this particular high action. Discovery of this use of the bit and the horse's susceptibility to it was made at least nineteen centuries before the foaling of Blaze, a prepotent Thoroughbred who founded the Hackney breed, a type uniformly possessing the ability to be taught to trot with higher action than other horses can readily attain. Chinese art as early as 125 B.C. depicts horses in harness and under saddle performing with Hackneylike action. The harness horses are controlled by reins that run through rings fastened to the ends of arms attached to the shafts. These arms extend to a point just higher than and slightly behind the horse's head. The bit is diffi-

Earliest representation of bit used to induce high action. Chinese inscription, 126 B.C.

cult to identify, but the noseband is tight, like that of a five-gaited horse whose rider uses a tight cavesson to prevent "cheating on the bit," in order to get high action (and some other results). The Chinese riders on the horses under saddle, of course, achieve the same effect by holding their hands high (no donkey, mule, ox, or other beast is structurally or nervously adapted to such use of or response to the bit!).

Again, it is the horse's adaptability to the bit that is an important factor in achieving the almost unbelievable and quite unnatural speed of modern race horses, especially of harness race horses. Proper bitting is a science almost occult in a harness race stable, and a knowledge of the peculiarity of each animal's mouth is studied carefully.

The gaits of the Saddle Horse and the Walker can be taught to some mules and, even, oxen; but the speed and elegance of the horse at the saddle gaits can never be approached by animals that cannot respond to the bit. Had the horse not been so constructed and so nervously strung up that he can wear and respond to the bit, he would not have been the great factor in man's development that he so unmistakably has been.

4. IN THE LAND OF SENNAAR

Those few respectable archeologists who have the temerity to hazard a guess tell us that the Great Flood must have occurred between 3800 and 3500 B.C. If they are right, Noah (or Noe, as the Douay spelling has it) must have taken aboard donkeys and bits to work them with when he was ready to start his spring garden again. There is some evidence to believe that what is now desert in Syria and Arabia was, for several centuries before and after the Flood, a fertile farm land in which donkeys were used to pull carts. We have little to indicate whether the farmers put bits in the mouths of the donkeys that pulled carts, but we do know that these ancient people of Sennaar (called also Shinar and, more commonly Sumer—see Genesis 10:10) used chariots. Their chariots were pulled by donkeys.

These Sumerians were certainly among the earliest users of

bits, though to date few details are available about the styles of those ancient donkey mouthpieces. The most definite information I have been able to find is in the twenty-four paintings that H. M. Herget made for the National Geographic Society of Washington, D.C. The Society states that these paintings, which the artist did not live to see published, were the result of painstaking research. The details of the paintings, states a spokesman for the Society, are based "upon the combined evidence of written and material remains and upon the smaller objects from Lagash and the finds from Ur."

One painting depicts Eannatuum, king of Lagash (a city in the Tigris Valley in Chaldea, the southern part of Mesopotamia), with his host of spear-wielding soldiers making a charge against the city-state of Ummah. The king, scepter in hand, standing beside the driver in a four-wheeled chariot, is obviously directing the charge of his foot soldiers. The chariot is drawn by four galloping onagers (line-backed wild asses). Each running donkey wears a heavy, halterlike headstall. Each is guided by a separate pair of reins (giving the driver quite a fistful to handle). Each rein is attached to its donkey by a ring located at the point where the heavy noseband of the headpiece touches the corner of the animal's mouth. Each ring is evidently attached to a bit, for though the corners of the mouth of each outstretched head are pulled back by the pull on the reins, the noseband is held firmly down to the corner of the mouth. It does not slide toward the top of the head as it would if it were not attached to a bit.

This probably marks the transition from the earliest form of headgear, which was simply a crude halter with a bosal-like nosepiece, to the earliest bits. This suggests the modern trainer's use of both hackamore and bit on the green horse that has been started on a bosal and is about ready to be ridden by bit alone. However, the Sumerian in the picture used only one set of reins and had his form of bosal firmly attached to the bit; whereas our modern trainer uses two sets of reins (or a hair rope and a pair of reins), one pair of reins going to the bosal and one to the bit; and the bosal is not attached to the bit.

5. THE HORSEMAN IN EGYPT

The donkey-using Sumerians began to decline in power shortly after 3000 B.C., but the donkey did not relinquish the stage to the horse in that part of the world until about 2000 B.C. At that time, the Babylonians succeeded the Sumerians. They and their successors, the Egyptians, had highly developed civilizations and accumulated sufficient wealth to attract the attention of their less civilized and less affluent neighbors who felt that the haves should be forced to share with the have-nots. Some of their neighbors in the mountains to the north were excellent horsemen, especially the Hyksos, about whom so little is known, and the Hittites. These horsemen invaded the rich valley. It is the Hyksos who are usually credited with introducing the horse to the Egyptians. However, they were probably able to succeed in their invasion because of previous victories enjoyed by the more

Chariot race scene from Panathenaic amphora, late fifth century B.C. Note studded band under jaw. The vase was actually filled with olive oil and presented to the winner of the race. From *The Birth of Western Civilization*, M. Grant, McGraw-Hill Book Company

powerful Hittites. And the Hittites were excellent horsemen.

The Hyksos did not last long in Egypt, but the horse remained. The Egyptians were so impressed by the animals that had aided the Hyksos to gain their temporary supremacy that the horse occupied a place of high honor in Egyptian society. In a tomb of the Eighteenth Dynasty, built about 1500 B.C., was found a horse that had been given an elaborate funeral. He was wrapped in bandages and encased in a huge coffin.

EGYPT DEVELOPS THE CHARIOT

The entombed horse had been buried with his saddle, so we know that the Egyptians did learn from the Hyksos something of the art of riding. However, they soon developed the chariot and found it a most useful article of war in their level country. The chariot in such terrain corresponded to the tanks and heavy artillery of more recent times, though it was useless in rough country and gave way to mounted fighters there.

However, though the civilized men of the valley to a great extent ignored the saddle in favor of the chariot, riding only to hunt and in some very special military maneuvers, they did not discard the bit. What evidence we have of the types of bits used by the Egyptians on chariot horses gives basis for the belief that they reflect the parallel development of horsemanship that had been going on in different parts of the world over a long period of time. Some Egyptians used bits quite similar to the primitive bits found in Russia, in the Swiss lake dwellings, and in Asia, which consisted simply of two sidepieces and a crosspiece. In each of these widely separated geographic locations, the bit was probably developed from some sort of noseband with no mouthpiece. (Even today in southwestern America, the bosal or jaquima is the favorite equipment to use on young horses. The jaquima has no mouthpiece and is the favorite headgear used by some of the finest horsemen alive.) [1]

---

[1] Early horsemen, however, did not learn the finesse of using the noseband most effectively, if we can judge from such meager sources as the Tassili frescoes, discovered in the Sahara in the mid-1930's by Henri Lhote, and

Some Egyptians, at least according to one careful archeologist, used a bit that was a transition between the noseband and the bit.

I have mentioned the paintings H. M. Herget did for the National Geographic Society, authentically detailed by a study of written remains and small objects from Lagash and Ur. One painting depicts King Thutmose III (1478 B.C.) in a two-wheeled war chariot. The bits he is using suggest something that might be made by combining a modern bosal and bar bit. The ends of the mouthpiece of the bit appear to be fastened to the rather snug noseband. The reins are attached where the ends of the mouthpiece are fastened to the noseband. The bridle has three cheek straps on each side. One of them is fastened to the noseband exactly where the cheekpiece is attached to a modern bosal, so that it comes down the cheek just missing the eye. Another cheek strap is fastened to the noseband where it is attached to the end of the mouthpiece of the bit. The third cheek strap is attached at the bottom of the jaw, about where the modern fiador, when used, is attached to a bosal. It is difficult to determine the function of the noseband, unless it is to keep the mouth closed. This would, as every polo player and five-gaited show ring professional knows, have a very definite effect on the response to a bit.

NUMIDIAN OXEN BIT INFLUENCE?

This design of bridle, with the multiple cheekpieces, may have come from some source other than the Hyksos or earlier mounted raiders. During the reign of Tutankhamen (c. 1361–1352 B.C.), Egypt had a viceroy in Numidia, which was evidently at that

Egyptian art of earlier discovery. They were prone to carry the band down on the nose so far that it cut off the wind, and they frequently lined it with studs or spikes. As late as the fifth century Greek artists depicted chariot horses wearing studded bands that were only partial nosebands. They went under the jaw and up each side of the face to a point just above and in front of the corner of the mouth. They were apparently held in place by a thong or strap over the nose and by cheekpieces much like those on a modern bridle. Sometimes the strap over the nose was decorative and possibly provided with a stud on top of the nose. These contraptions, though studded in a barbaric way, were obviously high enough to obviate the pressure on the soft part of the nose and the attendant interference with breathing seen in earlier similar devices.

time a flourishing Egyptian colony. This viceroy, Amenhotep, was apparently so successful in extracting riches from the colony that he was elaborately entombed. Wall paintings on his tomb depict Numidian princes bringing Egypt a great assortment of riches, from gold to the then highly prized giraffe tails. With them is a princess riding in a two-wheeled chariot drawn by two spotted oxen. Beside the princess is the driver of the oxen, a beautiful maiden, who holds in her outstretched hands four reins that are attached to headgear on the oxen. It is a bridle with two cheekpieces on each side. These support a tightly fitted contraption that goes through the mouth and over the nose. Nothing goes under the jaw. The device is wider where it goes through the mouth than it is over the nose. One cheekpiece is attached to it at the point where a bosal is attached to a cheekpiece. The other is attached just where the noseband enters the mouth. At this latter point, the rein is also attached. This bit and its bridle may have influenced the design of the Egyptian bridle with three cheekpieces. Whatever the origin, the triple cheekpiece survived for centuries and a modification of it is seen later supporting Greek and Roman bits with long curved sidepieces.

MARTINGALES AND OTHER INNOVATIONS

The Egyptians' use of the horse to draw the chariot created innovations in methods of using bits. There is no evidence that the Parthians, the Sarmatians, or other early riders of horses ever used anything that suggests the martingale, drawrein, or bitting rig. The mounted rider, of course, has the advantage of being able to raise and lower his hands to change the direction of pull on the reins; however, the driver of a chariot cannot shorten his reins and lower his hands if equine temperament or a punishing bit makes his horse come up in front at an inopportune time. How many horses reared and came over backwards

Detail from scene of the procession of the young Nubian princes in the tomb of Huy, Viceroy of Nubia, showing oxen gear (1400 B.C.). From *The Tomb of Huy,* by Davies and Gardiner, Egypt Exploration Society, 1926

Detail of a horse drawing a chariot, unusual because the chariot is drawn by one horse and the driver uses two reins running free from hand to bit (from a late eighth century B.C. amphora). From *The Birth of Western Civilization*, Thames and Hudson, London and M. Grant, McGraw-Hill Book Company

onto chariot or driver before the first Egyptian invented a running martingale (or his version thereof) we have no way of
knowing. Some of these early reinsmen used the drawrein, which
may have helped keep forefeet near the ground if the attachment of rein to harness was low enough.

In addition to martingales and drawreins, side- or checkreins
like the sidereins on a modern bitting rig or bareback circus
horse were used. We cannot be sure of the reasoning that
prompted such use, but the horse in the bitting rig cannot rear
away from a painful bit as readily as the horse who can thrust
his nose out and up.

Toward the end of the last century, a French Egyptologist
(and who could be more precise than a nineteenth-century
French Egyptologist!) published a book containing careful line
drawings of ancient Egypt and Assyria by M. Faucher-Gudin.
These depict details in the use of bits seen in many of the
wall reliefs, paintings, and other art. These seem to me to show
the use of the checkrein and the drawrein. The attachment of
the bit to a noseband precluded the gag action.

A rein on a chariot horse controlled by a drawrein was attached at one end to the harness or "collar." Then it passed
through a ring or slot at the end of the mouthpiece of the bit
(through which it moved freely), and then to the hand of the
driver.

In one of M. Faucher-Gudin's drawings, that of King Amen-
ophis IV, the solid attachment of the drawrein to the harness
is lower than is the ring on the harness through which the
driving rein slides freely in martingale-like fashion. In another
drawing, a depiction of the queen's chariot, the solid attachment is higher than the ring with the martingale effect. Possibly the fiery horses of the king were naturally higher headed
than those given the queen to drive!

Truth about Egyptian use of reins is beclouded by artistic remains of the time. For example, one illustration that has appeared in many books is the wall relief of Assurbanipal in his
chariot, hunting wild boars. Following him are attendants on
horseback. This picture supports the belief that while the Egyp-

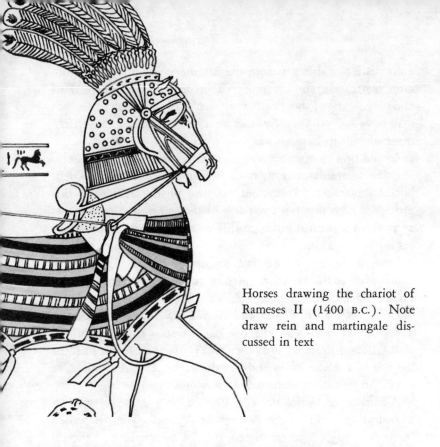

Horses drawing the chariot of Rameses II (1400 B.C.). Note draw rein and martingale discussed in text

tians preferred chariots to horseback riding, they did on occasion ride the horse, or at least their servants did. In many respects the picture is confusing and possibly one of the sources of some erroneous interpretation of Egyptian horsemanship. The details are so obscure that drawrein or checkrein, whichever it is, does not seem to go to the head of the horse on whose yoke it appears to be fastened. Instead it seems to be attached to the off side of the center horse of the three-horse team.

Whether or not the relief's obscurity of detail leads to the wrong impression of Egyptian horsemanship in this particular instance, it is certain that the Egyptians used two reins for each chariot horse. There is to date no evidence that they discovered the use of the Y-shaped rein for the driving of two or more horses (or the buck line so popular in multiple hitches on farms just before the tractor finally pushed the horse from the field).

With the Y-shaped rein, of course, the driver holds in his hand only two reins—the tails of the Y's. One arm of the Y goes to the outside bit ring. The other arm of the Y is a little longer (adjusted for length by careful hòrsemen exactly to suit the temperament and mouth of the individual horse) and goes to the inside bit of the other horse.

There is some conjecture that a few charioteers used only two reins. Each of the reins went to an outside bit ring on an outside horse. All other bit rings were attached by a short strap to the bit ring of the next horse. Such handling of bits of chariot teams is to be seen in Greek and Roman art, but I suspect artistic license is misleading us. Such rigging works fairly well in the deep and segregated South on overworked and underfed mules in the cotton fields. I have seen them worked with one rope line to each outside bit ring and the inside bit rings tied to each other by a short rope. (The teams were handled not by pulls but by jerks.) However, adapted though this kind of rigging may be to the South, it certainly would have caused havoc if used on the better-fed and warmer-blooded horses in royal chariots. At least it would have added to the drama of war and increased the business of the Remount Service!

Of course any tying of bit to bit would preclude the use of a drawrein (though not of checkrein), and there is considerable evidence to indicate that the Egyptians used the drawrein.

Tutankhamen, by one of the most respected Egyptologists, Christiane Desroches-Noblecourt, published in 1963, includes two very clear pictures of Egyptian chariots. One shows the use of a checkrein much like the checkreins that go from bit to surcingle on circus ponies to keep their necks arched (and to serve other purposes). The other picture shows use of a drawrein. In the first picture, King Tut is alone in his war chariot drawing his bow. His reins are around his buttocks, plowboy fashion. The checkrein is highly and colorfully decorated and could not possibly pass freely through a ring as a drawrein would. It is interesting to note that checkrein and driving rein are fastened not at the side of the horse's mouth but at the bottom of the noseband, where a heel knot would be on a bosal. The bridle in this picture has two cheekpieces on each side, one just missing the eye and attached to the noseband where a cheekpiece would attach to a bosal; the cheekpiece is attached to the noseband just ahead of the attachment of the reins. The noseband is very tight and very low—just above the nostrils.

The other picture is of a chariot in which the royal couple is leaving the temple of Aten. This obviously shows the check-rein. However, the bridle, the noseband, the cheekpieces and the attachment of the rein is the same as in the first picture. In this picture, the king has his reins in his hands, even though he is kissing the queen! It may be that in war the horses had to be kept on a checkrein because the charioteer had to give most of his attention to his bow and could not use his hands on a draw-

Relief of a race, marble sarcophagus (Rome, Circus Maximus, late third century A.D.). Note inside bit rings tied together. From *The Birth of Western Civilization*, Thames and Hudson, London and M. Grant, McGraw-Hill Book Company

Detail of horse pulling chariot which carried Teumaan's head through the Assyrian camp. Seventh century B.C.

rein; while in the second picture, the driver was handling the drawrein despite distraction. Could this be the forerunner of the one-handed automobile driver?

RUNNING MARTINGALES AND PLOW REINS

In many of the representations of mounted horsemen of ancient Egypt and Assyria unearthed long ago or recently, we see equipment that resembles modern running martingales. This is not surprising, because without exception representations of chariot horses and mounted horses of Egypt before the Persian annexation are all very high-headed. Most of the Mediterranean horses we see today are possessed of good head carriage, but probably the horses of that day carried their heads extremely high in response to the type of bits used on them. One fourteenth-century bit from Tel el Amarna, now in the Ashmolean

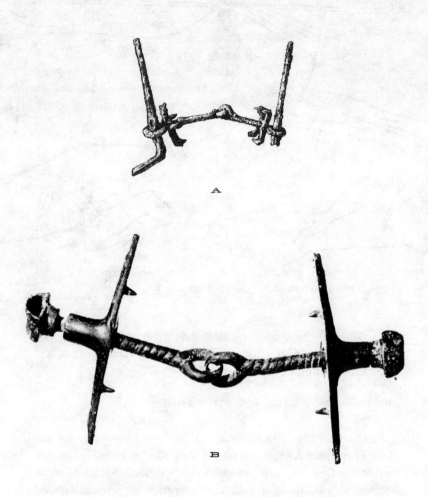

a. Scythian bit (fourth century B.C.). Jointed mouthpiece and spikes designed to compress the horse's lips and jaw from the outside
b. Egyptian bit from Tel el Amarna (1400 B.C.). Jointed mouthpiece and spikes designed to compress the horse's lips and jaw from the outside (Both from J. K. Anderson's *Ancient Greek Horsemanship*, 1961, University of California Press)

Museum at Oxford, has a mouthpiece exactly like a snaffle of today except that just inside the juncture of mouthpiece and sidepiece on each side there is a four-pronged claw. When pressure was exerted on the reins, obviously the prongs would jab the sides of the horse's mouth.

There is also a Scythian bit in the same museum. It is in a better state of preservation and shows clearly that reins were not attached directly to it. The mouthpiece terminates not in rings or anything else a rein could be readily attached to but in a short cylindrical stud that obviously went through a noseband and was held in place by a nut provided with a hole through which a thong could pass to tie the nut in place. This bit, like the one from Tel el Amarna, has a snaffle mouthpiece; however, the mouthpiece is made of very heavy twisted wire and it is provided with side plates bearing short spikes that press against the horse's mouth when the reins (attached to the noseband) are pulled.

Bits of the painful type like those in the Ashmolean Museum would certainly call for a running martingale. Also, they indicate that horsemen who used them employed the plow line or lateral pull, not a neckrein. Probably, when both hands were free, they held a rein in each hand. What is said to be the oldest representation of the horse in sculpture was done about 2000 B.C. It shows a horse ridden by a servant in breechcloth. He is holding his reins like a modern show ring professional in a hunter class —a rein in each hand, held short and well up on the horse's neck. This stable boy probably illustrates the current method of reining a horse. Neckreining probably did not come into use until the invention of the bit with leverage, the curb bit we call it, which did not occur until the dawn of Christendom (though some scholars call the early Celtic bits, which are without leverage but provided with metal jaw straps, *curb bits*).

NO TIE-DOWNS

Though painful bits and possibly the hot blood of Egyptian horses (forerunners of the Arabians of today) made martin-

gales vital to the control of both driven and ridden horses, no-
where can I find evidence of a standing martingale or "tie-down"
as they are called in the West today. Most representations of
chariot horses show use of the drawrein or of a ring on harness
or yoke located well below the height of the horse's mouth.

Egyptian sculpture, 2000 B.C., the first known representation of
man on horseback

Seventh century B.C. cavalryman using martingale

Through this ring the rein passes on its way from horse's mouth to driver's hand. This ring, of course, has the effect of a running martingale. Even mounted horses are usually shown with some device through which the reins run to keep the rein pull downward. Even mules wear such a device.

However, common though the running martingale was, I have seen no representation before the decline of Rome that resembles a standing martingale or tie-down. This is not surprising when we think of what a standing martingale would have done to the hot-headed little horses of Assyria and early Egypt with their spiked bits and nosebands. Today, though the most merciless of horsemen use nothing more severe than a wire cable noseband or a head chain, considerable damage is now and then done with a tie-down. The ancients, of course, did not seem averse to doing physical damage; however, a hot-headed, high-headed horse with a spiked bit would probably quickly render himself unfit for service if a standing martingale were added.

6. BITS AFTER
EGYPT'S DECLINE

In the thirteenth and twelfth centuries B.C., Egypt declined. In 730 B.C. Ethiopia conquered, probably taking back some of the wealth Numidia had in 1350 B.C. been forced to carry to Egypt—though the bit-wearing oxen and their beautiful driver had passed to oblivion. About a century and a half later, Assyria conquered Egypt. Persia annexed Egypt in 525 B.C. Two hundred years later Alexander the Great, using the kind of horsemanship and bits of which Xenophon gives us exact written description, rode Bucephalus in his conquest of the Persians. This sequence of events brought Ethiopian, Assyrian, Persian, and Greek bits and horsemanship to Egypt.

Of all these peoples, only the Assyrians seemed to use gear to keep the bit pull constantly downward. Anything resembling

The horses of the defeated Susian cavalry are a part of a triumphal procession led by Assurbanipal through the gates of the capital of Assyria (c. seventh century B.C.). Note similarity to the primitive American Indian thong around lower jaw.

a martingale is absent from the representations of Persian horses, mounted or in chariots. In all probability, the coarse-headed horses of the Persians did not require such gear. (The coarse head of these later horses, in contrast to those of early Egypt and Assyria, is attested by the name of Alexander's horse—Bucephalus. It is translated as "oxhead" or "bullhead"—the language of ancient Greece did not include the distinction between ox and bull.) In contrast to the heavy-headed horses of Persia and of the cavalry of Alexander, the horses of the Numidians and the Moors were a different type. Slender is the adjective most frequently applied to them in the brief references historians give. The Numidians were never a major power in world history, but they seemed to be battle prone and crop up frequently in historical accounts of pre-Christian wars. It is regrettable that we have so little definite information about their horsemanship, for it may be that from them and the Moors, who usually fought in wars in which the Numidians participated, we got the jaquima and the horsemanship that goes with it.

Seventh century B.C. Assyrian relief showing jaw-pinching action of side piece of the most popular bit of the period in the Mediterranean area. From *Ancient Greek Horsemanship*, J. K. Anderson, University of California Press

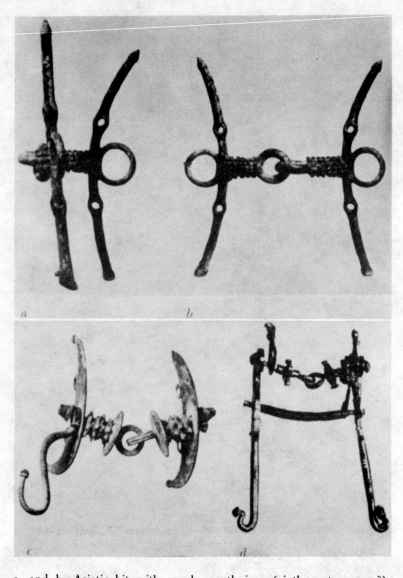

a. and b. Asiatic bit with rough mouthpiece (sixth century B.C.?).
c. Greek bit with "hedgehog" or echinii (fourth century B.C. or later).
d. Celtic bit sometimes miscalled a curb (early third century B.C.) from
J. K. Anderson's *Ancient Greek Horsemanship*, 1961, University of
California Press

An account of one of the Grecian battles gives an amusing description of Numidian horsemanship. These Africans dashed toward their enemy in a seemingly poorly organized array. The foremost horsemen appeared to have little control of their mounts. Some of them fell off. Their opponents were so amused at this that they let down their guard and enjoyed the spectacle. At that moment, the Numidians, who had been using the clowning forefront as a ruse, dashed forward and mowed down their enemy.

Harold Lamb, in his very readable *Hannibal,* says, "The Numidians and Moors rode without reins—using both arms against a foeman who had only one arm free if he guided his horse with reins." I have searched in vain for a description of the bits or headgear used by these Africans. I still suspect that they knew the secret of the jaquima, for a jaquima-trained horse, better than any other, could perform as theirs are reported to have done. However, even the frescoes of the Sahara, so recently discovered by M. Lhote, indicate no bits other than those similar to the ones I have already described in use in Egypt and elsewhere.

If the Greeks learned anything about bits and their use from the Numidians, they have left no record of it. They were, until the time of Xenophon, users of Egyptian, Celtic, and Scythian bits, and a few variations of their own.

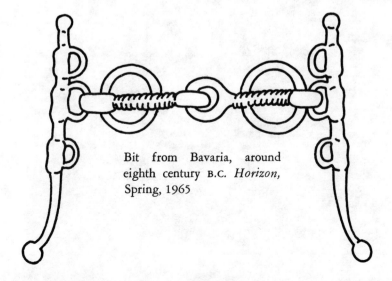

Bit from Bavaria, around eighth century B.C. *Horizon,* Spring, 1965

One of the earliest bits found in Greece, said to have been made in the Bronze Age, is jointed like our snaffles. Each part of the mouthpiece or cannon ends in a loop for attachment of a rein. The loop passes through a wide hole in a cheekpiece provided with spikes that dig into a horse's mouth when the reins are pulled. The cannons are twisted, suggesting that the bitmaker was imitating a bit with mouthpiece of rawhide or fiber.

Persian bits from Persepolis (before 331 B.C.). From *Ancient Greek Horsemanship,* J. K. Anderson, University of California Press

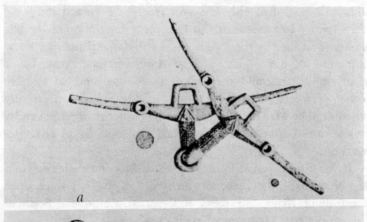

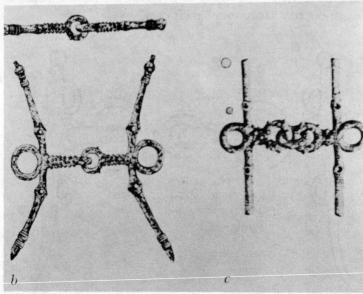

Similar bits of the same era found in Egypt have cannons that pass through snug tubes. Each tube is part of the cheekpiece. The cannons rotate freely in the tube and have D-shaped ends for attachment of reins. Obviously, the Grecian bit, with its very loose juncture of cannon and mouthpiece, would allow the entire inner surface of each cheekpiece, with its spikes, to bear on the sides of the horse's mouth when reins were pulled; whereas the Egyptian bit with its tubular juncture of cannon and cheekpiece would cause the edge of the cheekpiece to bear on the side of the mouth. Whether this is the intentional application of Greek intelligence or happenstance, we shall never know. Certainly the Egyptian bit was more difficult to make.

EARLY GREEK BITS

The Greeks, at least as late as 700 B.C., used bits with the long crescent-shaped cheekpieces so common in Egypt. Like the Egyptians, they used a bridle that held the cheekpieces at right angles to the horse's mouth so that when reins were pulled, the lower ends of the cheekpieces pinched in against the jaw. However, the Greeks soon got away from the dropped noseband used in conjunction with such bits by their early neighbors. Also, whereas the Egyptians used three cheek straps on their bridles, two fastened at either end of the long cheekpiece of the bit and the center cheek strap fastened to the outer end of the cannon, the Greeks used one cheek strap that divided into three branches just above the bit. As time elapsed, the cheek straps divided into only two branches. By the time Xenophon appeared, a period I shall discuss later, the divided cheek strap had disappeared, as had the pinching sidepieces of the bit. This, as we shall see, was not a change to more humane bits—just a shift of the place of torture. The *psalion,* described earlier in this book, was also used in Greece but was certainly going out of style by the time of Xenophon.

Prior to the Persian Wars, Greek bits were not usually made with roughened, spiked, or studded mouthpieces. Such details they seem to have taken from the Persians and developed into

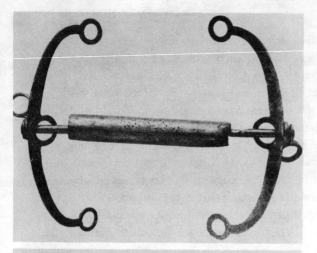

a. Bronze bit from Olympia (550-490 B.C.). The straight bar mouthpiece is enclosed in a length of narrow tube which revolved.
b. Iron bits from Olympia (550-490 B.C.). Both from *Ancient Greek Horsemanship*, J. K. Anderson, University of California Press

an entirely new kind of bit, as we shall see presently. One interesting mouthpiece the Greeks used as late as 500 B.C. is the great-grandfather of our roller mouth bits. The mouthpiece of that bit is a straight bar or bolt that passes through a cylinder that rotates freely. A rough hand could do considerable damage with such a bit because the cylinder is shorter than the bolt, just enough so to cause the ends of the cylinder to dig into the inner edges of the bars of the mouth if the bit was jerked sidewise. As the neckrein was not in use at that time, the side jerk on the reins was probably common.

This roller mouth bit had the conventional crescent-shaped sidepieces with holes for attaching the three cheek straps or the three branches of a cheek strap. However, the crescent is not quite as long as many of those seen with jointed bits, and the jaw pinching action for which the long crescent was evidently originally designed could not operate with a bit that was not jointed. In other parts of the world (at the time the Greeks had a roller mouth bit) fantastic, pain-causing mouthpieces were in vogue. Jointed bits with spiked or studded cannons, twisted cannons, bits with mouthpieces made of large spiked rings, and other contraptions were used. With all this infinite variety, however, the disks of classical Greece did not appear.

 ## 7. BITS OF
THE GOLDEN AGE

By the time Xenophon, follower and friend of Socrates, joined
the army of Cyrus (401 B.C.), the chariot was no longer a military weapon. It was, however, an important part of Greek life.
Nine-mile chariot races were an attraction in Olympia. The
bridle with three cheek straps to keep the long side bars of the
bit in proper position for pinching the jaws had given way to
the single cheek strap with two or three branches. The side bars,
or cheekpieces, of the bit had been shortened, so the bit's pinching action on the jaws was negligible or nonexistent. Reliance
on the bit's action on the bars of the mouth, the inside of the
mouth, then became the important thing.

USE—HANDS AND REINS

Users of the earliest bits, those with thong mouthpieces and smooth mouthpieces, could ride with rather sluggish hands. It is a fair guess that reins were a part of the rider's balance, as illustrated by the modern jockey's method of riding. Even the invention of the claws and spikes on the sidepieces would not prevent the constant keeping of some pressure on the reins. Many a fancy buggy horse in the days before Henry Ford had chronic sores on the outside corners of his mouth. The ones with the worst sores were usually the ones that were the pullers —the ones that had hard mouths and had to be driven by a man with stout arms! A few of them were cured of the habit of pulling. This was done by expert horsemen who used light hands and leather or rubber or smooth metal bar bits. They provided such bits with round leather guards at the outer ends of the cannons of the bit. These guards relieved the pain on the corners of the mouth. Then the horsemen would use a technique sometimes called "snatching them back"—steady hold on one rein and quick pull on the other at the proper instant.

Like our old buggy horses that leaned into the painful driving bits, horses of early days probably took the constant pain and were ridden with some pressure on the bit at all times if they were sufficiently well fed to have animation. The earliest piece of horse sculpture, that of an Egyptian slave (in breechcloth) riding without saddle, shows the straight wrist and hands hanging onto the reins in good modern English fashion. The date of the statue is said to be about 2000 B.C.

Information about bits and especially about methods of using them is too scanty before Xenophon for any attempt at an exact correlation between hands and bits. However, the kind of dull pain caused by some bits tends to make a horse pull into the bit, to bore into the pain until he seems to become insensitive to it. Other bits, some of them no less humane, cause a quick, sharp pain, when used by a quick, deft hand; such bits can make a light mouth and can be used with a light hand. Very generally speaking, as the ingenuity of bitmakers centered more on trick mouthpieces that brought sharp pain to the bars of the mouth when reins were pulled and depended less on studded nosebands and spiked cheekpieces, hands became lighter. There are some representations, such as one of Lybian horsemen, that show the use of the slack rein, the light hand, and the bent wrist that betokens the light hand.

MODERN CLUES TO AN ANCIENT PUZZLE

To shed light on this change of bits from the early ones that worked on the softer tissues outside the mouth to later ones that worked more on the sparsely covered bones of the bars inside the mouth—a change that was accompanied by a shift from relatively taut reins to the relatively slack reins and light quick hands so emphasized by Xenophon—let us glance at some modern training methods. The use of the rawhide braided hackamore (or a synthetic substitute) in the training of horses to be used in any kind of competition demanding quick starts, stops, and turns has today spread all over the United States. However, there are two distinct ways in which the hackamore is used. One method employs a fairly loose hackamore, so loose in fact that it necessitates the use of a fiador to keep it from slipping off the horse's chin. With this method, the action of the rawhide is on the nose just above the soft cartilage. Occasionally a trainer will wrap the front of the Bosal (noseband) with wire to make its action more severe. This method tends to result in a horse that works with his head low. He tends to carry more of his weight on his forehand than does the horse trained by the method I shall discuss presently. He can be ridden by a rider with a more sluggish hand than can the one trained by the method next described. In fact, such a horse can usually be ridden by the rider who constantly keeps a little pressure on the reins.

Another method of using the hackamore for training, using pressure on the lower jaw rather than on the nose, calls for a much less loose bosal. The noseband (bosal) is just tight enough so that the instant pressure is released the rawhide ceases to press on the *bottom* of the lower jaw. It is tight enough to insure that at the instant pressure is applied to the reins, the rough shanks of the bosal come into contact with the lower jaw. This method, used by an expert, results in a horse that works with hocks well under him, and carries much of his weight on his hind quarters when he is doing fast work. While he has extreme flexion at the poll, his head tends to be higher (taking congenital factors into consideration) than the head of the horse trained with a loose hackamore that works on the nose rather than on the jaw. He must be ridden with a light hand and a slack rein. (This is not the slack rein of the inexperienced. The slack is slight, and it conveys the rhythm of hand to horse's mouth as well as the rhythm of horse to hand of rider.)

These two methods may point up a difference that seems subtle, but it is extremely important. In the first method, the action is on the more or less rounded nose of the horse. The part of the bosal that presses on him is rounded. Compared to the lower jaw, the tissue pressed upon is soft; and it is often used by the horse to push against things. The lower jaws are no more sensitive than the nose, but there is little covering over those sharp bones. The bosal is not rounded where it comes into contact with the jaw. It is V-shaped. The point of contact is very small—it does not cover a wide area as does the part over the nose.

In the Southwest of this country a frequent sight is a young horse being ridden with a rawhide hackamore working cattle, either in the cutting corral or the roping arena, executing the quick turns, starts, stops, and reverses such work entails. To the uninitiated bystander, the reins seem always slack.

One form of Western humor practiced upon visiting horsemen from the East illustrates the great difference between the use of the hackamore and the use of the bits of so-called educated horsemanship of Europe and eastern United States. It also gives some insight into the difficulty modern scholars have in understanding Xenophon's use of the bit. Fortunately this joke on the accomplished horseman from the East is much less common today than in the days of the Old West, when horses were cheap and the chance of spoiling a colt was not too high a price to pay for a little fun.

The usual setting for the joke was a Sunday afternoon small gathering of hands on a ranch watching the hossbreaker work a few hackamore colts. If there happened to be a dude guest at the ranch who was a horseman, the horsebreaker would rope out a young animal that was coming along pretty well on the hackamore. He would demonstrate its good rein and stop. Then he would invite the guest to try out the young horse. The moment the new rider gathered his reins, the horse would start to whip its head from side to side or indulge in some similar defense against the foreign hand. If the guest was of an aggressive temperament and sensitive about his equestrian standing, a first-class rodeo performance would soon ensue. It is surprising that such affairs usually ended with no more physical harm to the rider than a tumble in the dust.

If the guest was a likable fellow and horseman enough to recognize instantly that the trouble was on his end of the reins, and if the horse had been trained on the loose hackamore that works on the nose rather than on the jaw, things might turn out differently. An immediate request for help would probably be responded to by some terse advice about "letting go of his head." If the newcomer had a good pair of hands and a keen mind for interpreting laconic advice, he could start his education in the use of the hackamore on the spot. If he could learn to ride the young horse around the corral, execute a few turns and a moderate stop, he was a success, and everybody was almost as happy as if he had been thrown.

If, on the other hand, the colt had been trained on the snug bosal that works on the bottom of the jaw, it is very doubtful that even the best of eastern horsemen could have had any success. A seasoned hackamore horse and a sympathetic teacher are the requisites for the first lesson in the use of the hackamore.

It is quite probable that the hands of Xenophon, like the hands of Tom Lea's Cantu, were light beyond the comprehension of modern horsemen. At least this assumption gives me the only clue to Xenophon's use of his bits with their disks and *echini,* or hedgehogs, as they are sometimes called.

8. XENOPHON'S BITS AND THEIR USE

Classical Greeks, Xenophon included, evidently knew nothing of the hackamore, but their bits demanded the quick, light hand of the hackamore reinsman of old California. There was no leverage involved in those bits of Socrates' time. Reins exerted a direct pull on the bars, or (if noses were ever thrust out) on the corners of the mouth. There was undoubtedly some other pressure, especially if the rider was inept or sadistic, for the mouthpieces of Xenophon's bits were extremely complicated affairs. The few reasonably authentic examples that have come down to us, or that have been dug up for us, have sidepieces that resemble those of previous eras. They were made of bars or flat pieces of metal, crescent-shaped or S-shaped. The small rings, much like those on a modern Pelham for attachment of lip straps, two on each cheekpiece for the attachment of the branches of the cheekpiece, were closer to the center of the crescent or S than were some of the much earlier bits. However, they did keep the crescent or S at right angles to the mouth.

The mouthpiece, composed of two jointed cannons, at outer extremities went through the sidepieces and through the stems of hooks to which the reins were attached. The cannons ended in conical buttons that acted like rivet heads to keep them from pulling out of hook stems and sidepieces. The cannons were either covered with or composed of three or four spiked rollers extending from cheekpiece to large disks that surrounded the cannons right next to the joint that held the two cannons to-

Hellenistic frieze, showing open mouth induced by "hedgehog" bit. Temple of Halikarnasos. The Bettmann Archive

gether. Whether the spiked rollers, called *echini* or hedgehogs, were a rigid part of the cannon or revolved upon it like the rollers of a modern roller-mouth Hanoverian Pelham, is hard to determine from the corroded remains. Undoubtedly, the disks did revolve. The juncture of the cannons resembled that of our snaffles, but the interlocking rings forming that juncture were sometimes much larger than any on our snaffles. On one specimen we can see attached to the juncture of the cannons six interlocking light rings. They evidently lay on the horses's tongue (if he could keep it under such a complex bit) for him to jangle. They served a purpose similar to that of the player toggles (sometimes called keys) on English mouthing bits. How a "play pretty" could attract any attention from a horse with his mouth full of spikes and disks is very difficult to determine.

XENOPHON'S *THE ART OF HORSEMANSHIP*

The earliest complete book on horsemanship that has survived the mass burnings, pillages, and wars that have been the chief concern of man, the "higher" animal, for the centuries he has graced this planet, is Xenophon's. Its title is translated as *The Art of Horsemanship*. This book has been around since sometime before 372 B.C. However, it was not until 1894 that we had a translation by a man who was both a scholar and one who had some knowledge of horsemanship, Morris H. Morgan, Ph.D. Dr. Morgan was a Harvard professor, but one must send to England for his book. It was, fortunately, republished in 1962 by J. H. Allen & Co., Ltd., 1 Lower Grosvenor Place, London, S.W.1. The good doctor, like some contemporary American scholars, is not quite clear on a minor point or two because his knowledge of horsemanship is largely confined to English and European equitation. So he occasionally fails one who is looking for clues to the distinctive features of the unique bits and extremely light hands they require, not to mention the open reins and a few other very minor points significant to riders experienced with horses trained to the slack rein, the jaquima, or the spade. However, the copious, clear notes sup-

a. Greek muzzle from grave in Boeotia (fourth century B.C.)
b. Fourth century Greek bit with discs and echinii, discussed by Xenophon. The side pieces are turned in the picture to show their S shape. When worn they lay flat against the outsides of the horse's mouth. From *Ancient Greek Horsemanship,* J. K. Anderson, University of California Press

a

plied by Dr. Morgan and his excellent translation are by far the best source we have of knowledge of classical horsemanship.

We learn from Xenophon that the model horseman of his day used two bits. However, he did not use the two bits simultaneously as does his modern English counterpart. Each man, says Xenophon, must have two bits, "one smooth with the disks of good size," the other with "the disks heavy, and not standing so high, but with the *echini* sharp." *Echini* is the name of the spiked rollers on the bit. It sounds quite fitting to modern ears because it is the name we use for a marine creature, or family

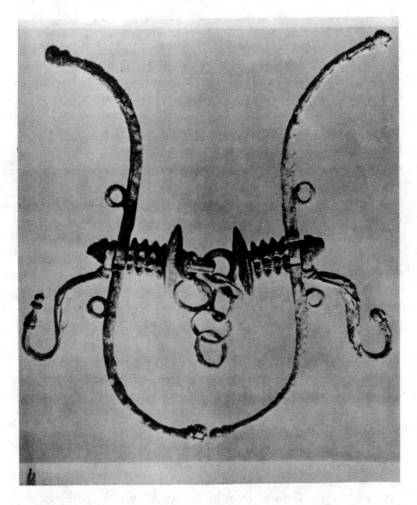

of creatures, that is well provided with spikes. What Xenophon means by smooth, Dr. Morgan tells us, is not what we think. To the Greek horseman a "smooth" bit was one provided with *echini* having rounded rather than sharp points.

The "rough" bit, Xenophon says, is to train the horse to do those things which he should. The smooth bit will be such a relief to him that he will do them on it willingly. However, should he forget and be a little loath to do right, he can be returned to the sharp *echini* for a short term, a sort of refresher course. All this is slightly suggestive of the horse of our time trained with hackamore and spade, though many of them are trained without any pain whatever—and there are horsemen who claim that the horse trained with a spade can never be ridden with another bit (one such in my stable will work beautifully on snaffle, light Pelham, or full bridle if asked).

Xenophon would be at home among old Baja California horsemen in a discussion of stiff- versus loose-jawed bits. The modern stiff bit, the one cast or forged all in one piece without any joints, did not exist in his tack room. However, he warns against the use of what he calls a "stiff" bit. In his lexicon that means one having a snug fitting joint. He says the joints should be "broad and smooth—roomy, not tight." He advocates the light hand, saying in one place, "The moment he acknowledges it [the bit] and begins to raise his neck, give him the bit."

"Smooth bits," says Xenophon, "are more suitable for such a horse [a high-mettled one] than rough; but if a rough one is put in, it must be made as easy as the smooth by lightness of hand."

Another clue to the fact that Xenophon used a hand on the bit as light as that of a hackamore reinsman in his insistence that a horse that dislikes the bit is worthless. In his words, "Willingness to receive the bit is such an important point that a horse which refuses it is utterly useless." It must have taken much skill to use a hedgehog bit without making the horse detest it.

Other evidence that the Greek horseman used his bits in a manner suggestive of the hackamore reinsman is the kind of performance he obtained from his horse. All Greek art depicts horses working on their hocks; that is, in a state of extreme collection. Dr. Morgan tells us that Simon, of whose work we have only mere fragments and a few allusions by Xenophon, wrote of training the horse in "the demipassade, the volte, and the oblong career with sharp turns at both ends." Such feats are stylized versions of some of the things a hackamore and spade bit horse does so well. While the classical Greek seemed to pay as little attention to the quality of the walk, the trot, and the canter as does the modern Western rider, he did insist on training at both leads of the gallop.

9. BITS OF ROME

With the rise of the Roman Empire, the role of the horse changed. The change is suggestive of that in the role of the horse with the advent of motor vehicles in our own time. The utilitarian importance of the horse declined, and his use in sport and for theatrical entertainment increased. The cavalry was no longer a major part of warfare. Such cavalry as the Roman Empire did use was that of its "auxiliaries." These were the so-called barbarian peoples. Hence, at the rise of the empire, the bits of Rome were the bits of the entire Mediterranean world. Such primitive ones as the ornate, elongated pieces of bone held at right angles to a horse's mouth by divided cheek straps and joined by a thong mouthpiece were undoubtedly still in use by some of the auxiliaries. The *psalion,* described earlier, bits with

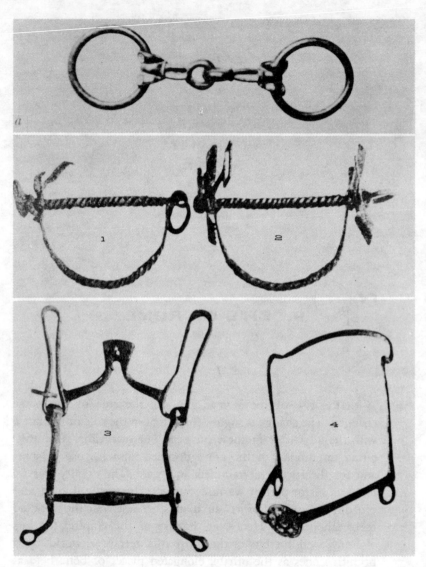

a. Celtic ring snaffle with two-piece mouthpiece (early first century A.D.)
b. (1 and 2) bits with twisted bar mouthpieces used by Celtic auxiliary
cavalry in Roman service (second century A.D.). (3 and 4) bit and metal
cavesson or psalion (Roman, second century A.D.). From *Ancient Greek
Horsemanship,* J. K. Anderson, University of California Press

clawed cheekpieces, bits with jointed mouthpieces—some rough and twisted and some with rollers—all helped build the Empire.

Up to the time of the rise of the Roman Empire, no bit that employed the principle of the fulcrum, as does our curb bit, had been used in the Mediterranean world. Also, I can find no evidence that any horseman of that world ever used the neck-rein. With the change of the role of the horse from that of utility to that of sport and theatrical spectacle, there was certainly a use for the curb bit. Several scholars assert that the Romans did invent the bit to fill the need. However, what such writers describe and depict as a curb bit lacks the distinctive feature of our curbs. It does not involve the lever principle at all. These Roman curb bits were simply metal bar mouthpieces, usually twisted to make them rough like our twisted wire bits, attached to U-shaped metal bands that went under the horse's jaw. Obviously, if the horse was running with his nose out, as race horses do, any pull on the reins would pull the bit upward into the flexible corners of the mouth. Also, the metal band under the jaw would be pulled upward toward the larger part of the jaw. Thus both mouthpiece and jawband would cause pain.

If a writer wishes to call such a bit a curb, I suppose he has a right to do so; but he is using the word for a kind of bit very different from our curbs. Perhaps there is a feeling in his breast that any bit that works on the outside of the lower jaw is a curb. If so, we must call many of the bits of ancient Assyria, Egypt, and elsewhere curb bits. For they were designed to pinch the lower jaw. The mouthpiece was jointed. The sidepieces were extremely long and held at right angles to the mouth by triple cheekpieces. When the reins were pulled, the lower arms of the sidepieces pinched the lower jaw.

Some such bits survived into the Roman Era. Other Roman bits were modifications of those older ones. However, the Egyptians and other earlier peoples used dropped nosebands and studded nosebands in conjunction with the jaw-pinching bits. The Greeks and Romans frequently used the single cheek strap divided just above the bit. Often they used no noseband at all, though one depiction of Marcus Aurelius in a chariot shows dropped and studded nosebands used without bits.

It was not until Romans invaded England and Flanders that they knew of the use of the fulcrum in bits. Why this bit grew entirely out of the use of the massive horse of Flanders and the Great Horse of England is quite puzzling. Surely the clawed bits the nomads of the steppe country used on their tough ponies could cause enough pain, if pain was the goal in controlling a horse—as it was for many centuries. The hedgehog bits of Xenophon's cavalrymen would seem to be just as effective horse controllers as any long-shanked curb, but as far as any evidence I can find indicates, the true curb bit is an invention of northern Europe.

One writer, Sir Walter Gilbey, Bart., in his *The Great Horse* insists that England is the home of the Great Horse and all that goes with it. If so, England may well be the author of the curb bit. Sir Walter claims that two distinct types of horse (and several subtypes) developed in England. One of them was the small, easy-gaited horse highly regarded as a saddle animal in England until the seventeenth century, typified by the Hobbies and the Galloways. These showed the conquering Romans the joy of a gaited horse, and the amble very early became a popular gait for a riding animal in Rome. The other horse developed in England, says Sir Walter, was the Great Horse. And it was with the use of this horse that the curb bit came into being.

In partial support of his thesis that England saw the origin of the Great Horse, Sir Walter quotes Caesar's account of the forces in England that resisted his conquest.

Most of them use chariots in battle. They first scour up and down on every side, throwing their darts; creating disorder among the ranks by the terror of their horses and noise of their chariot wheels. When they get among troops of [their enemies'] horse, they leap out of the chariots and fight on foot. Meanwhile the charioteers retire to a little distance from the field, and place themselves in such a manner that if the others be overpowered by the number of the enemy, they may be secure to make good their retreat. Thus they act with the agility of cavalry; and the steadiness of infantry in battle. They became so expert by constant practice that in declivities and precipices they can stop their horses at full speed [possibly thanks to the curb bits]; and, on a sudden, check and turn them. They run along the pole, stand on the yoke, and then, as quickly, into their chariots again. They frequently retreat on purpose, and after they have drawn men from the main body, leap from the pole and wage unequal war on foot.

Sir Walter says that to draw those huge, clumsy convoy chariots at speed and "force a way among disciplined cavalry" required horses of great size and substance. The maneuverability of the teams also, he feels, points to the temperament of the Great Horse, progenitor of the Shire.

Other evidence of the Great Horse in England during the first century is found on British coins of that time. They bore the likeness of a horse, and it was clearly a horse of draft type. Unfortunately for our purpose, the coins do not show a bit, but evidence is ample that the curb bit was used with the massive horses of Flanders and Normandy before Caesar left his native land to conquer all Gaul, and the Britons undoubtedly used similar bits.

Along with fair-haired Britons to sell as slaves on the streets of Rome, Caesar took home with him the curb bits and some of the large horses of the northland. After his conquest of the North, curb bits were used in the Mediterranean world, and the infusion of blood of northern horses increased the size, bone and feet of some of the horses of Spain, Italy, and other lands of the South.

In their chariot races, which were several miles in length, Roman horsemen used the bits of the old types. In racing mounted horses, they also used bits without leverage; but mounted officers, especially on parade duty, began to use the new bits brought back from the North, the true curb. The long-shanked curb is the bit seen in all early Christian art depicting mounted horses.

10. BITS AFTER THE FALL OF ROME

Man evidently first conceived of the bit as a device to inflict pain. If a little pain got results, then more pain would get bigger and better results—so seemed to be his thinking. Claws and studs on the outside of the mouth were devised and elaborated. Spikes, rollers, disks, and other ingenious devices of torture were invented by what Mark Twain called "the damned human race." Simon and Xenophon, the Greeks, brought the false dawn of a new day when man would realize that there is a better way to get along with a horse than torturing him to make him perform.

Xenophon credits Simon with the statement, "What a horse does under compulsion is done without understanding; and there is no beauty in it either, any more than if one should whip and spur a dancer."

Xenophon himself says, "If you reward him [the horse] with kindness after he has done as you wish, and punish him when he disobeys, he will be most likely to obey as he ought."

Xenophon eliminated the claws on the outside of the mouth. He also did away with the spiked and studded nosebands and the dropped noseband that cut off the wind and punished the soft part of the nose. However, he used a bit that filled the horse's mouth with spikes and sharp disks. It is understandable that he warned, "You must refrain from pulling at his mouth with the bit."

While the use of torture on the soft tissue on the outside of a horse's mouth declined after the fall of the Roman Empire, the use of the curb spread over the world. The painful effect of the lever was augmented by elaboration of the port into fantastic devices of torture. Prior to this time no horseman of the Mediterranean world had thought of a bit with the reins attached to an arm or shank that would cause the mouthpiece to turn in the horse's mouth. When Caesar brought home such a bit, horsemen were quick to see that if the mouthpiece was designed with a high port, turning it would cause pain; better still, if a high "spade" were added to the port, results would be increased. Then claws and spikes were added to the spade. One particularly ingenious Spaniard, several centuries after the curb had come to the Mediterranean area, devised a bit that combined the leverage (curb chain included) of the curb, the high port, the spade with claws, and the disks and hedgehog of Xenophon's day!

THE RING AND THE SPADE

While the variety of bits in the early Christian Era seems almost infinite, actually there were, with two exceptions, no innovations of mechanical principles. The claws and spikes were older than the pyramids. Jointed mouthpieces, stiff mouthpieces, rollers, and disks were copies or elaborations of ancient designs. The ports and curbs were importations of old designs of Europe or Britain. One innovation involving an entirely new mechanical principle was the ring bit. The exact place of its origin is unknown. The date can only be stated as "early Christian." This bit is one of the two of that time that are still in use today. Of course, our modern English curb and its Western version employ the principles of the elaborate curbs of Caesar's day; and our snaffles and bar bits are simplified versions of the bits of the ancients, but we have stripped them of all the torturing claws, disks, and spikes, so they are hardly recognizable as descendants of the old bits. The ring bit is practically unchanged. The early ones were decorated on the sidepieces, but the structure was that of the bit to be seen today on practically every horse ridden by the Basque sheep- and cattle-herders of certain parts of western United States. These Basques are so gifted in the handling of animals that the ranchers in areas where Basque herders are to be found will employ no others, so the local merchants must stock Basque merchandise. One storekeeper in northern Arizona recently told me that he had such difficulty in obtaining for his customers ring bits from wholesalers, though several houses list them in their catalogs, that he contracted for a supply from a local blacksmith.

The mouthpiece of the ring bit is a straight bar. From its center rises a port, or spade, some two or three inches high. It terminates in a short tube that is parallel to the mouthpiece. Through this tube passes a ring just large enough to go comfortably around the horse's lower jaw. The sidepieces of the bit are a rigid part of the mouthpiece, either welded to it or forged as part of it. Each sidepiece forms a right angle with the mouthpiece, extending downward from it at least four or five inches. Small rings for attachment of the bridle are located at the top of the sidepieces, at the point where they form right angles with the mouthpiece. The lower extremities of the sidepieces are provided with small rings for the attachment of reins. Pressure on the reins causes pressure on the mouthpiece, and because such pressure turns the mouthpiece and its port, through which runs the ring encircling the jaw, it also presses the jaw ring against the horse's chin groove. Because the port is shorter than the sidepiece, or shank, of the bit, the lever-and-fulcrum action of the bit magnifies the pressure on the bars of the mouth. The jaw

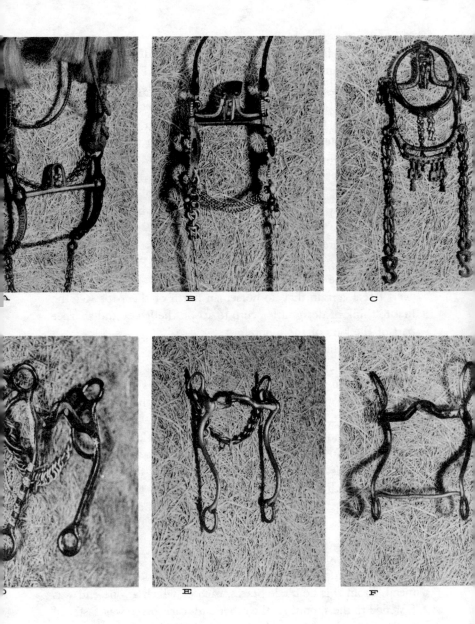

a. Mexican half-breed bit; b. Santa Barbara spade; c. Mexican ring bit; d. Monte Foreman pelham; e. Original Walking Horse bit; f. U. S. cavalry bit of frontier days. Ring bit and cavalry bit courtesy of Troy's Western Store, Scottsdale, Arizona

ring, like the braces of the spade bit, to be discussed later in this book, fits into the corners of the mouth and keeps the mouthpiece low on the bars, where it will act severely.

The ring bit is the only one employing lever action that can be used well with the plow rein or lateral pull on the rein. As the Mediterranean peoples did not use the neckrein, Caesar's introduction of the curb must have created some difficulty. We are left wondering if some wise horseman of Africa or Arabia did not invent the ring bit to solve that problem (it is today called variously Turkish ring bit, Moorish ring bit, and Arabian ring bit.)

Though there can be little doubt that the use of the lever in bit design originated in Britain or northern Europe, tangible evidence of the designs of those first curbs is very scanty. However, I feel certain that no horseman north of the Alps was the first to think of designing a curb to act on the lower and sharper part of the bars of the mouth.

Not until the curb bit was taken by Caesar's horsemen back to Rome did any horseman design a curb bit that would act consistently on the lower part of the bars. This design was the second of the two mechanical innovations in the bit design in the very early Christian Era.

As gaited horse trainers (and some others) know, the lower a curb hangs in the mouth, the more severe its action. However, even if a bit is hung so low that it just misses the bridle teeth, an upward pull on the reins brings it up onto the broader and less sensitive part of the bars. Somewhere in northern Africa or Arabia, a horseman "improved" the design of the bits brought back from the northland. He changed the port into a kind of spoon or "spade" two or three inches long. Then he twisted some wire (copper wire is used today) around a tiny rod of metal. From this he made braces, each of which at one end was fastened to the spoon. At the other end, each brace was fastened to the cheekpiece of the bit about one half inch above the point where the mouthpiece was attached to the sidepiece. Each brace was curved downward, following close to the spoon until it got below the first molar tooth. Then it turned outward and ran parallel to and just above the mouthpiece until it reached the sidepiece. Since the mouthpiece was below the brace, and the brace could go no higher in the mouth than the corners of the mouth permitted, the mouthpiece was kept constantly a little lower in the mouth than that of the old-style curb.

This first spade bit with braces was the parent of a variety of bits based on its principle. Some spoons were provided with rowels, others with spikes.

Today the spade bit is still with us, though its use in the hands of any but the especially gifted and deft is justifiably condemned. Those few experts achieve a subtlety and brilliance of performance seldom equaled. They probably use the spade as its first designer intended, not as metal to work on the roof of the mouth as the ignorant and cruel think it is to be used, but as a most subtle means of communication between horse and man—the spade or spoon giving the horse great aid in transmitting his part of the communication to man. (I have never seen a spade-bit horse under a *gifted* spade-bit rider show any sign of mouth distress or discomfort—no head tossing or getting behind the bit.) Today the spade-bit man uses not the elaborate variations with their torturing rowels and spikes but the simple spade described above. There are some modern bitmakers who design a spade without decorations and without the wide cheekpiece that prevents lipping the bit. However, the most popular spade today is a replica of the old bits of the East. Even the Moorish or Arabic designs are still reproduced on the cheekpieces.

A MODERN SPADE STORY

The day before writing this discussion of the spade bit I drove into the town of Prescott, Arizona, for grain for my horses. When in Prescott I rarely resist my inclination to visit the saddle shop now operated by Chick Logan on Whiskey Row. Chick owned and launched on their road to fame some of the greatest of the early entries in the American Quarter Horse Registry— Bar Fly, Frosty, Red Joe, Cowboy, Sleepy Joe, Dusty Hancock, and others. I can sometimes induce him to talk of those days.

That day I dropped in at the saddle shop mainly to have a look at the exquisite hand tooling that I knew Ardith Forsgran was doing on a trophy saddle to fulfill one of the many special orders that keep Chick and Ardith very busy.

After admiring the almost-completed trophy, I moved across the shop so I would not impede the work of Ardith or interfere with Chick's endeavor to find the exact kind of a saddle pad a very particular customer was wanting. My attention was caught by a much-used but well-preserved bridle hanging on the back wall. In it was hung a loose-jawed, Santa Barbara spade bit. I was examining on its cheekpieces the intricate design of stars, crescents, and other things suggesting the Orient when Chick, finished with his particular customer, came over to me.

"That's been on some good ones!" he affirmed, seeing my interest in the bit.

Then he told me of one of those "good ones," nameless here to avoid embarrassing the living. The horse was trained to perfection and then purchased by a California buyer, for Chick had defected from Arizona to California by the time this horse was trained. Chick said he had told the new owner to use a mild curb on the horse. (The rider not skilled in the use of a spade can get all the performance he is capable of getting from any horse if he will use a mild curb on a well-trained spade-bit horse.) However, the new owner had seen Chick use a spade, so he bought himself a spade bit as soon as he got his new purchase home.

In a few days Chick saw the horse. The language used to express that horse's performance is not appropriate here. I did not ask Chick if the horse ever recovered from the spoiling, for I know that, like the horse that was made to balk by an ignorant teamster in the old days of draft horses, no horse spoiled by misuse of a spade bit ever completely recovers.

Probably eighteen hundred years ago Arabian, Moorish, or Turkish horses were trained and spoiled in the same way on the same kind of bits that I saw hanging in Chick Logan's saddle shop.

When Caesar's last soldiers left Britain, isolated bits of land that had been protected by Roman military installations became strongholds of whatever overlord had means to protect them from marauders. Walls and moats became part of the means of protection, but the Great Horse was a very important part of the protection afforded by the lord. The feudal lord developed armor to protect himself and his horse. He devised rein guards, some of them very cumbersome, to prevent the cutting of bridle reins, a favorite technique for rendering the horseman helpless in battle.

These great lords of Britain did not stoop to the learning of A B C's. They neither read nor wrote. We have no record of their use of bits or reins. Some of their bits have found their way to museums. And great, cumbersome, long-shanked curb bits they were. We have no way of knowing for certain whether they used them by neckreining or by lateral pulls. However, it is difficult to imagine how those long-shanked bits could have been used by the lateral pull method, and the reins with their heavy guards would have been very awkward to use by the plow-line method. When some inventive Briton replaced the rein guards with chains, it is doubtful that he found the plow line more useful.

BITS AND SOCIAL STATUS

For centuries after Rome left the northland, the Briton or European who could use the bit was the man of power and privilege. We might even say the man who could use the *curb* was the man of power and privilege, the protector and master of other men. There was no human achievement more valued or respected than horsemanship. These masters of men, in Britain, were Saxons; and the horses they used, according to Sir Walter Gilbey, were the type of the Great Horse, progenitors of the Shires, the Suffolks, and the Clydesdales. The serfs, though in battle they fought on foot, undoubtedly made some use of the hardy ponies, some of which still run wild in remote parts of England. The serfs, mainly descendants of the Picts, the Scots and the Celts, who were the natives overrun by the Saxons and by the Romans, undoubtedly used the bits of their ancestors. The earliest Celtic bits of which we have any remains were bits without leverage. So the distinctions of caste might be said to be the Great Horses and curb bits of the Saxon lords and the small easy-gaited horses and the snaffle bits of the serfs. From the latter came the "ambling palfreys" for the ladies and retainers to use as transportation. Centuries later, a priest describing the livestock of Ireland, wrote of a Hobby, a highly esteemed type among these small horses, "So easy was his movement that a man could carry while mounted a glass full of liquor and never spill a drop."

These easy-gaited small horses were not adapted to the use of the curbs worn by the Great Horses. Their gait was a congenital one not induced by severe bitting. It did not disappear as an inherited trait in English horses until the seventeenth century.

11. THE RISE OF "EDUCATED" HORSEMANSHIP

Though the huge horse from Flanders reached his apogee with the full flowering of chivalry and declined in favor as it withered, horses ridden by nobility and royalty depicted in art of the Renaissance were of stocky and sturdy build. The bits they wore were curbs with shanks often more than double the length of those on our curbs, highly decorated and fantastically curved. Probably the use of four reins, as we use them with a four-ring Pelham bit, came about thanks to the Riding Establishment of the Tuileries, founded by Louis XIV, which became the most famous school of equitation in Europe, according to Lady Apsley in her *Bridle Ways through History.*

With the decline of the age of jousting in heavy hardware, so amusingly described by T. H. White in *The Sword in the Stone,* education began to rear its egg-shaped head. "Educated horsemanship" became the fashion in the courts of England and on the Continent. Hands that were clever at using the bit began to wield the pen. At this time a sharp division among horsemen sprouted, one that has continued to grow even into our own day. Until very recently, the lines of this dichotomy corresponded with those of social class.

At the outset, educated horsemanship was the province of nobility and royalty. The other side of the coin (which we hardly dare call "the riding of the illiterate," for today probably more books are being written about other kinds of horsemanship than about educated horsemanship) was the province of the country squires. Educated horsemanship, then as now, was concerned with the proper way to do a very definite number of rigidly specified things on horseback and to do them with a very definite and specified type of horse. Horsemen of the other school are prone to consider riding as an adjunct to or means of doing almost anything that seems desirable. They are a little apt to champion their horses, even today, as practical, useful creatures and to scoff at the artificiality of the performance of the horses of the educated school. (To tell them that as soon as we put a horse inside a fence we are doing something artificial to him is worse than useless.) The extremist of the educated school maintains that his is the horse par excellence, the horse to be respected above all other types, and that he gets from his horse all the performance that is of any value to any sane human.

From each of these schools we get bits and uses of bits that prove of value. From the educated school we learned the use of the curb and the cavesson in certain very special kinds of performance, along with other valuable techniques. From the other school we learned much about the use of the snaffle and the full bridle to get extended movements, though the educated very early capitalized on it and added to our knowledge.

BOOKS APPEAR

A few books about horses were written before the invention of printing in the middle of the fifteenth century. Some of them were published later. At least one mentions bits. It was written by the painter and architect, Leone Battista Alberti, and was published some eighty years after his death, which was in 1472.

The first book that records "a complete and reasoned method of equitation," according to Vladimir S. Littauer in his excellent *Horseman's Progress* (1962), was one written by Federico Griscone, published in Italy in 1550. Even though the sixteenth century saw the dawn of educated horsemanship, bits of the time were probably the most brutal the Christian world had known. Some had mouthpieces so fantastic that some of the horse's teeth had to be removed to accommodate the bit. Others were used with spiked straps around the outside of the mouth. One such bit is pictured in Littauer's *Horseman's Progress.* It is reproduced from the 1608 German edition of Griscone's book, *Gli Ordini de Cavalcare.* Such were the bits of the "complicated manège

In the seventeenth century curb bits of the European riding schools became so complicated that sometimes some teeth had to be removed from the horse's mouth to accommodate the bit. From *Horseman's Progress,* Vladimir S. Littauer, Van Nostrand

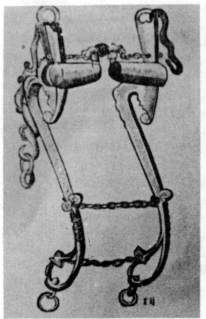 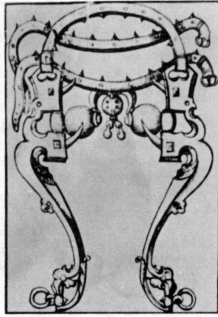

riding, with its slow, dramatic, highly collected gaits" during the Renaissance. Manège refers either to the great riding halls of the times of Pluvinel and the Duke of Newcastle, of whom we talk later, or to the kind of horsemanship taught in them.

PLUVINEL

Possibly the best and certainly one of the most widely esteemed horsemen and teachers of nobility and royalty of the period was Pluvinel de la Baume, Director of the Royal Stables of Henry IV and subsequently Governor to the Dauphin, who became Louis XIII. King Louis made him *Ecuyer* (Instructor in Horsemanship to His Majesty). Later he became Ambassador to the Netherlands.

Pluvinel was a particular man about bits. He, like others of his time, used long-shanked curbs. They were all single-rein bits but of many designs. He did not like the painful bits of many of his predecessors. He insisted that any bit should be so designed that it did not hurt a horse's mouth when used by a *cavaliere.* He insisted that for each horse a bit should be selected that suited the conformation of its mouth and tongue as well as its disposition. He said that he himself used only a dozen or so bits.

Lady Apsley writes that she feels that those bits of Pluvinel were not so severe as they looked because "horses were trained to go very much behind their bits—and I fancy a lot was done with neckreining." Certainly any use of the plow rein, or lateral pull, on those long-shanked curbs with their complicated mouthpieces would have wrecked a horse's mouth.

Though Pluvinel did not use the snaffle, he did make much use of the cavesson. He used it to "set the horse's head" by tying it in the proper position. He also used the cavesson to tie the horse to pillars, either to a single pillar or between two, depending upon the lesson to be learned. This teaching of the movements of manège, some of them at least, by tying the horse between pillars and whipping him, could probably not have been done on any but the chunky, draft-type horse of the day—though we are told that he had Oriental blood in his veins. Some of Pluvinel's predecessors were so fond of the whip that a conventional part of the equipment of the riding school was a servant (*chambrier*) who carried a bundle of "switches."

THE DUKE OF NEWCASTLE

I find it impossible to pin down the invention of the modern snaffle. Also, the way in which the straight shank, now a rigid convention on all English curb (Weymouth) bits, was made popular is a puzzle to me. The straight shank is much less practical than the S-shaped one, for it demands the addition of a lip strap, and it will pinch the corners of the mouth against the chain unless it is adjusted with great care. However, though we can not establish the inventor of the modern snaffle and the conventional English curb, one man outstanding in the history of horsemanship, William Cavendish, Duke of Newcastle (1592–1676), probably did as much to establish the popularity of these bits as any man who ever lived.

A member of Charles II's Privy Council, Newcastle retired to Antwerp during the exile of Charles and lived in the house of Rubens' widow. While in Antwerp he established his famous riding school and wrote a very influential book, *A General System of Horsemanship*.

After the Restoration, Newcastle returned to England and retired, then turned his attention to horses. He established a racecourse and wrote another book, *A New Method to Dress Horses* (1658). His use of bits is a revelation of such use in all the Western world and a clue to the origin of many new uses, as his own statement about himself indicates:

I have practiced ever since I was ten years old, have ridden with the best masters of all nations, heard them discourse at large and tried their various ways; have read all the French, Italian and English books and some Latin ones and in a word all that had been writ upon the subject good and bad; and have bestowed many thousands in horses, have spoiled many and have been very long learning of this art of Horsemanship.

Newcastle is the first noted horseman to do away with what Lady Apsley calls "the pistol cannons" of the old curbs with their disks, studded rollers, and similar devices (which Pluvinel felt would not hurt a horse in the hands of a *cavaliere*), and to do away with the double pillars (still in the use in the Spanish Riding School of Vienna, where a special horse has to be bred to endure the type of training given), and to do away with the *chambrier,* the servant supplying whips. Yet this man who probably brought more humanity to the use of the bit than any before him wrote:

The horse must know you are his master; that is, he must fear you, and then he will love you for his own sake. Fear is the sure hold, for Fear doth all things in this world. Love little, and therefore let your horse fear you.

Perhaps Newcastle's apparently paradoxical aspect is not quite as hard to understand as is that of our contemporaries who claim to be humane and to love their horses yet hire trainers to do the things so condemned in *Sports Illustrated* (which condemnation finally resulted in a conviction, for which there was a fine of $25—paid by the trainer!). I recently watched a female acquaintance of mine work out her Walking Horse in a training arena. Finished with the mild workout, she handed her horse to an attendant. I watched while he cross-tied the animal and took off its boots. Under them were chains beneath which blood was trickling from chronic sores. My acquaintance stoutly maintains "I love my horses! and pay the highest price to the best trainer so that they shall have good care." Another acquaintance dotes on her Thoroughbreds yet sends colts to the track to be crippled every year.

Perhaps among horsemen we are apt to find paradoxes and should not be surprised at them. So let us return to our seventeenth century horsemen.

Newcastle did use a single pillar for teaching some of the "airs," but he used hands on the cavesson reins after the first preliminary work. He considered the results of the older methods "wooden," and advocated suppling the horse's shoulders by using the cavesson "tied my way"—reins held in the rider's hands rather than being tied to the pommel.

Not only was Newcastle the first to use the cavesson (in those days a very heavy piece of harness, indeed) with a rein held in the rider's hand rather than fastened securely to the saddle; he was also the first horseman of record to use a drawrein, which he called "the sliding rein." This was what he meant by "the rein tied my way." He fastened the anchored end of the draw-rein firmly to the saddle at the height of the rider's knee. From there it passed through a great ring on either side of the ponderous cavesson. The ring was located just in front of the bit, which was of course attached to the bridle and entirely independent of the cavesson. From its passage through the cavesson ring, the drawrein went to the hands of the rider, whose left hand also held the very slack reins of the curb bit.

So successful was Newcastle's use of the drawrein that it soon spread to all major countries of the Western world to be used alone or as an occasional supplement with the curb bit.

12. ORGANIZED RACING CHANGES BITS

While racing was known in England before the time of New-castle, organized racing developed in his century. It is per-missible to assume that its evolution was similar to that of Quar-ter-Horse racing in our own day. Our first racing Quarter Horses in the forties were often of the heavily muscled stock horse type, such as the famous Dusty Hancock, who, it is said, created a problem by spreading his hind shoes off his feet with the power-ful thrust of his haunches at the starting gate. Today it is im-possible to tell a racing Quarter Horse from a Thoroughbred without looking at his registration papers (which often bear the same names of ancestors as do those of the papers of a Thorough-bred). Racing in England in the seventeenth century soon es-tablished the popularity of the light-legged, hot-blooded horse (in sharp contrast with the type depicted by Velasquez in the same century as mounts of nobility). It also taught such intelligent horsemen as Newcastle the value of letting a horse get his weight forward. This, of course, he cannot do on a curb bit, unless the rider cuts off the reins or "throws them away." Racing also precludes neckreining. Today, when polo is played on race horses rather than on handy ponies, some players carry their reins across their palms and guide their ponies by lateral pull.

Race horses appeared in Newcastle's day wearing snaffle bits, and snaffle alone, without nosebands on the bridle. One type in use then I have seen on American race tracks. It is still listed in the catalogs of all major saddlery firms as the full cheek bit. The cheekpiece of that bit is a bar about five inches long, at the center of which is a ring about two inches in diameter for attachment of reins and bridle. The cheekpiece bars suggest those of old Egyptian bits, though the bars of the modern ones are not held at right angles to the horse's mouth by a triple cheek strap as were those of Egypt.

Though Newcastle learned the use of the snaffle from the race track (if, indeed, he did not invent it), he insisted that unless a horse had been trained to respond to the curb "he would never go well on the snaffle." With whatever bit, Newcastle used a tight noseband, "which made the bit lie in its correct place." Always the noseband was lined with double leather. It is probable that our full bridle seen in the hunting field today, with its broad cavesson, is a reflection of Newcastle's equipment, though the cavesson on our bridles is but a vestigial remnant of that double-leather lined one of the Duke of Newcastle.

RISE OF THE THOROUGHBRED

The change in bits from the gruesome ones of the Middle Ages and the Renaissance to the less fantastic ones that have been in fashion for two or three centuries was not instantaneous. It paralleled the change in the type of horse idealized. England led the world in the development of the race horse, now called the Thoroughbred. She was to the world, in this development, what the tiny bluegrass region of Kentucky was to America. So to get an insight into the great change in bits and their use after the Renaissance, a few facts about the development of the English race horse are a prerequisite.

Up to the time of the first organized racing in England, the most highly prized horses of nobility and royalty ranged in type from the Great Horse of England to the Spanish horse depicted by Velasquez and other artists, a horse with a breast like a pouter pigeon and a general conformation suggesting an enlarged Shetland. Outside the elaborate establishments of the manège supported by the nobility, England had been developing, more or less by chance and convenience, a type of horse that was to be a cornerstone of the Thoroughbred (even though the later proponents of the breed were to claim as its foundation three Oriental horses). Of these English horses at the time of the Restoration Newcastle wrote:

Certainly the best English horses make perfect horses for hunting or riding and to hawk, and some are as beautifuul horses as can be anywhere, for they are bred out of all the horses of all the nations.

As the breeding of this light-legged horse began to gain favor, supporters of the Great Horse presented a petition to the king begging him to prevent the type of horse "fit for the defence of the country" from dying out. However, the Duke of Montrose (possessing first-hand knowledge of the horsemanship of Italy and France) had shown the efficacy of light cavalry by conquering all of Scotland with it for his king, and the argument of the Great Horse fans was out of date.

Charles II set up the best breeding establishment that the Island had ever beheld. Some authorities claim that he sent abroad for his mares, which were to go down in history as the famous "royal mares." But one of the most reliable books, *Royal Studs,* maintains otherwise. Then, as now, the label "imported" impressed the fashionable set; and owners of progeny of the Royal Mares probably did all they could to establish foreign ancestry of their stock. Some of those mares undoubtedly were imports, but others (possibly the best) were of English stock.

The first volume of the *Stud Book,* the oldest record we have of pedigrees of English race horses, was not published until 1808. It includes the pedigree of a horse called Counselor, bred by a Mr. Edgerton in 1694. The *Stud Book* gives his pedigree as tracing to imported Oriental stock on both sides within three or four generations. However, the Duke of Newcastle in his *A New Method* includes this horse among a list of horses of the manège none of which were the light-legged, hot-blooded Oriental type; and I would trust the word of the Duke in preference to that of a compiler of records in the employ of his betters. Such discrepancies support the supposition that fashion rather than fact credits Oriental blood with so much influence in the development of the English race horse. Surely, if Oriental horses played as big a part in the development of the new breed as some think, Oriental bits would have come over with the horses now and then. But there is no trace of the ring bit or the spade in England that I can discover, to say nothing of the thorn bit and others of atrocious design that were used in the Orient then. Parts of the world into which the Spaniards brought foundation stock of North African, Egyptian, and Arabian extraction still use equipment of the Near East. In our Southwest, the spade is still in use. Gauchos of the Argentine ride with no bit at all, using the dropped noseband of ancient Egypt, dropped so far in fact that it hangs across the nostrils. But I can learn of no sign of Oriental bits in use now or at any other time in England.

The superior qualities of the English race horse and the bits that developed with him were not the result of importation (though some beneficial dilution of blood did come from the Orient) but of selection and emendation of stock and bits already existing in England. We might have to except the use of the snaffle (often very correctly called the bridoon) as a matter of invention, but bits of the ancient Celts could well be considered the great-grandparents of the snaffle, or bridoon.

HUNTING INFLUENCES BITS

The race track was not the only cause of the change in type of horse and the change in bits in the seventeenth century. Fox hunting, long known in England, rose in fashion and status during the reign of Charles II to become the sport of royalty and nobility. The bits of the manège were as out of place on a fox hunt as they were on the race track. A horse could never keep in view of the hounds while behind the bit, and manège horses must be. So great was the disfavor toward the old curbs that the straight, simple shank now seen on all English curbs evolved. Even with such a curb, a horse could not take fences at a hunting pace. No horse will extend himself to the utmost if he feels pressure from the curb; so the double, or full, bridle came into fashion. As the princely sport increased in popularity and fashion, there were members of hunts who rode only to hunt, as they do today. These were the ones who "rode the bridle," hanging on by the reins to compensate for their own lack of balance. Perhaps they are the ones responsible for the first realization of a very important fact, namely, that it is the hand of the rider rather than the mouth of the horse that demands a special bit.

To my mind, the greatest bit ever devised to meet the problem of the poor hand on the good hunter is the one sometimes called the Irish bridoon. Its very name suggests that it may have been invented by a clever Irish groom to protect the mouths of hunters ridden by some resident magistrate when he rode a-hunting. It also suggests that the snaffle, or bridoon, descends from the jointed bits of the ancient Celts. The cannons of this snaffle are of such a large diameter that they will do the least possible harm to the bars or the corners of the mouth. The joint is smooth and loose. The sidepieces are large, flat rings, more than double the diameter of those usually seen in double bridles.

MY HUNT WITH AN IRISH BRIDOON

My most vivid memory of personal experience with an Irish bridoon is of a hunt with the Rocky Fork hounds. While I was not a member of the Rocky Fork Hunt Club, located near Gahanna, Ohio, I owned a farm some six miles away on which I was breeding horses and cattle. There was some virgin timber on my farm, and always a fox den or two. The hunt frequently met at my place, and I was always a welcome guest of the hunt.

Since boyhood I had been friends with F. Everson Powell, M.F.H., and Major Harry Brown, the moving spirits of the club. To this day, though Master Powell and Major Brown have long since passed to foxhunters' paradise, I have not learned the truth about how that ride on an Irish hunter wearing a big bridoon was planned to make me the butt of a good joke, or who planned it. I still suspect Harry Brown. At least, it was he who called me by phone one day during cubbing season to say that he had acquired an excellent, imported Irish hunter and would like to have me try him in the field.

What a horse that hunter was! He stood near seventeen hands, with a heart girth almost beyond belief. I thought of Kipling's "the mouth of a bell, a heart of hell, and the head of a gallows tree." It fit the horse except for the "heart of hell," unless the enduring quality of Satan's province makes it appropriate.

On a strange horse, I like to use a full bridle. Then I am prepared for any kind of a mouth. However, the big hunter was saddled and bridled when he was presented to me, and I felt it would be a discourtesy to ask for a change of gear. In his mouth was a big Irish bridoon. One pair of reins was free. The other ran through martingale rings almost as high as the horse's withers.

Hounds drew cover in a patch of timber that was being logged off. I thought it an unlikely place to look for fox. Off to my right, hounds' voices began to sound interesting. As I jogged in that direction a few steps, I felt as if I was bumping down a flight of stairs, so rough was the gait. Well behind the Huntsman, we stood quietly a few minutes. Then "Gone away!" sang out just as it would during regular hunting season. Hounds were in full cry. The great horse between my legs was electrified. Though his jog had been horrible, he galloped like a dream horse, with supernatural power. The woods were cluttered with slash and treetops from the logging operation. My mount, huge as he was, showed me he could find a way through in spite of the rough going. I jammed my cap down and clamped my head against his neck. Suddenly before us was the trunk of a great oak recently felled. Over it was the only way through. The big head of my horse thrust forward, giving three mighty yanks on the reins with that big bridoon. Whether they were to ask me for a free rein or to get me as far forward as possible, I'll never know. If free rein was what he wanted, he certainly got his wish, for I threw him the slack and clamped the ends of the reins across his neck with both my hands tight against its sides and my head tight against it not far behind his.

That oak trunk, kept off the ground at its outer extremity by branches, must have been well over a four-foot obstacle and solid as Gibraltar. Of course I had read about how in some parts of Ireland hunters are trained to push the top of a dike with their hind legs when jumping a bank and ditch obstacle, but this was no time to recall academic knowledge. The great gelding took off like a bird, but in mid-air the mighty haunches drove those hind feet at the top of that oak log like a catapult. The roughest chiropractor in the world never gave a snap of a neck equal to the one I experienced at the thrust of those haunches. Somewhere, off to my left, I heard muffled laughter where I knew one of the whips was riding. I am still certain he and some others that day anticipated that I'd come a cropper, but my riding all over the big bay's neck evidently afforded some amusement. Had I not had the ends of the reins crossed over the gelding's neck and grasped firmly on either side of it, I probably should have lived up to their expectations.

Judging from the mighty thrusts the bay gave on the reins before his take-off, I am sure that Irish bridoon gave him complete control of the situation and that he could have taken that or any similar jump without difficulty even if I had sat back and hung onto the reins. Yes, the Irish bridoon, I'm sure, was devised for the horse's sake to be worn when m'Lord So-and-So, who only rides to hunt, was up.

13. BITS USED WITH HEAVY VEHICLES

The rise of organized racing and formal foxhunting in the seventeenth century were accompanied by changes in bits and in styles of riding. They also dealt a blow to the preference for the lateral-gaited horse as transportation. However, the death blow to the easy-gaited horse as a means of transportation was dealt by the rise of the wheeled vehicle. The horse in the manège did not use gaits other than the stylized walk, trot, and gallop; but for transportation the easy gaits, seen today only in our five-gaited horses and Walking Horses, were considered the only proper ones for a horse transporting ladies and gentlemen before the seventeenth century. A trotter was called a "bone shaker" and considered fit only for servants to ride or for use as a pack animal. By the end of the seventeenth century, the pacer (the name for a horse that did any gait other than walk, trot, and gallop) was passé in England.

Many of the easy-gaited horses were highly prized in the American colonies. The Canadian Pacer was valued very highly and crops up in the pedigrees of the early American Saddle Horses. The fame of the Narragansett Pacer is legendary.

The rise of the popularity of the trotting horse was certainly due as much to the rise of the use of the horse in harness as it was to the increase of racing and hunting; for, contrary to Hollywood versions of the horse pulling a buggy, the gallop is not suited to harness use. Any horse in harness that broke into a gallop was making a mistake. Even in harness races, the horse that breaks always loses time.

BITTING RIGS AND DUMB JOCKEYS

To prepare the young horse for the use of harness bits, the biting rig and dumb jockey were often used. Versions of these devices had been used in the manège, but they were modernized and techniques of using them became more humane. An excellent book written in the latter half of the nineteenth century describes the use of the bitting rig and dumb jockey. I quote in part this description in *Driving for Pleasure,* by Francis T. Underhill, published in 1896.

The bitting harness is employed in the first breaking in of a colt. If it is left on the horse for an hour or so daily when in a loose box, it will accustom him to the finding of a comfortable position for his head when held in restraint, and will tend to develop the necessary muscles.

The bit should be a snaffle, with iron keys or tassels attached, and should be dropped comparatively low in the mouth, for in this position it has a tendency to encourage flexion and yielding.

After a couple of weeks of treatment with the bitting harness, during which time the pupil may be given leading exercise, it is well to begin the use of the dumb jockey and cavesson. The modern dumb jockey is made with two hard-rubber arms, each extending upward and outward from the centre of the pad; these are furnished with eyes into which the side reins, etc., can be fastened. These side reins are made partly of rubber, so that they will yield to a comparatively light pressure, thereby to a great extent obviating the danger of a "dead pull." The horse very soon finds that his head and mouth are more comfortable and easy when he yields to the pressure exerted by the elasticity of the rubber, and consequently drops his head into the position which gives him that relief. This is exactly similar to the result which a man with excellent hands is able to accomplish, and which is so much to be desired.

The cavesson is no more nor less than a rigid noseband to which rings are attached on the front and sides, and into which the "lounging" reins, side reins, or other straps can be buckled at the pleasure of the breaker, in order to accustom the horse to restraint aside from that of the bit. This is a most useful instrument in the hands of a skillful person, but it can be made very injurious when improperly applied.

Having given the horse several days of the dumb jockey, he may be led or lounged with the cavesson. It will be noticed that the treatment has already brought him into better balance. An intelligent use of soft ground and thick straw, with occasional logs among it which can be seen, will add very materially to his action and carriage.

INNOVATION OF SLIDING CURBS

One of the first innovations that was probably a result of the use of horses to pull carriages for gentle folk was the sliding action of the curb. It was achieved in either of two ways. In one, the ends of the mouthpiece were the shape of a ball or cylinder. The sidepiece or shank passed through a hole in these ends of the mouthpiece. Each shank was a little larger just above and below the part that passed through the mouthpiece. The small part passing through the mouthpiece was from one-quarter to a half-inch longer than the diameter of the mouthpiece, so the latter could slide up and down on it for a fraction of an inch.

Another kind of sliding action was achieved by having each end of the mouthpiece protrude through a slot in the shank and end in a button shaped somewhat like a rivet head, which kept it from coming out of the slot. The slot was long enough to allow the mouthpiece to slide up and down a quarter of an inch or more.

The popular sidepiece of the earliest coaching bits was flat below the juncture of the mouthpiece and shaped like the numeral 7. There were usually two slots for attachment of the reins in the long part of the 7 so that the severity of the leverage could be varied to suit hand or mouth, as I shall explain by quotation later. Some bits were provided with a loop that attached at its bottom end to the angle of the 7 and at its top to the sidepiece midway between the juncture of the mouthpiece and the upper extremity of the sidepiece, which was a loop or ring for attachment of the cheekpiece of the bridle. When the reins were used in this loop, of course, the bit had no leverage action and functioned like our bar bits used often on roadsters or harness race horses.

Of course, not all coaching bits were of the sliding action type. However, rigid bits were in the minority. Most of those that did not have sliding action of one kind or the other were made so that the cheekpiece turned freely where it passed through the end of the mouthpiece. In the late nineteenth century a bit called the Liverpool was invented. It was much condemned by the foremost authority of its day "because even when the bars are pivoted they do not turn freely so that the two inside bars are usually pulling at an angle on the bit, and do not give an even pull on the horses' mouths." This criticism is reminiscent of Xenophon, who condemned the use of what he called "stiff" bits—bits that were jointed, of course, but whose joints did not move freely.

The popularity of jointed and sliding bits for harness use at a time when the rigid English curb was coming into its very firm and permanent place in polite society throughout the Western world arouses curiosity. Xenophon claims that with the flexible bit the horse "is always after the part that is getting away from him in his mouth" so that he "drops the bit from his bars." Many modern horsemen have a similar reason for their preference for "flexible" bits, called loose-jawed bits today in the

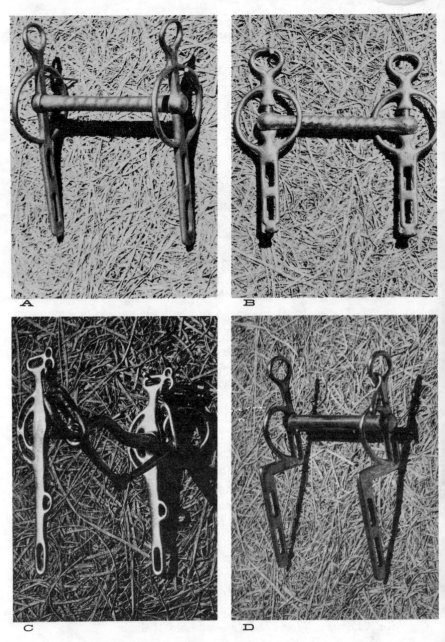

Coaching and heavy harness bits: a. Liverpool (rigid shank); b. Liverpool (swivel shank); c. ported curb with bearing rein bit attached; d. Ashleigh. From Harry Haynes's collection, Denver

West. They claim such bits prevent "dry mouth," that is, the habit of keeping the mouth tight shut with no mouthing of the bit. This habit they associate with a hard mouth and general resistance to training. It may be that the men who used the horse under saddle did not need a flexible curb to keep the horse mouthing the bit, because with the full bridle the snaffle with its loose joint serves the purpose of keeping the horse "after the part that is always getting away from him in his mouth." Certainly most horses have a tendency to play with bits when wearing a full bridle. There are, of course, today several types of English riding curbs with sliding mouthpiece, but most of the riding curbs in the early days of formalized hunting and organized racing were rigid.

I fancy that the chief reason for the popularity of the sliding action of early coaching and carriage bits was that they made a noise and the mouthing of the bits made the horses look animated. The practical advantage of the loose-jointed or "loose-jawed" bit as it is used today in the West is that it facilitates riding with the slack rein. Just as the finely trained horse rarely has to feel the spur because he gets the message the instant the muscles of the rider's leg flex—long before the heel moves toward the side of the horse—just so, reins rarely have to lose their slack on the finely trained Western horse because the slightest movement of the hand is translated through the slack rein into a movement of part of the very flexible bit and the horse gets the message long before there is any need for taking all the slack out of the reins. As one old-timer puts it, "If he's a good horse, you ride him with weight of the reins."

This is the kind of riding, I feel sure, that Xenophon did with his bits equipped with *echini,* or hedgehogs, and disks. I seriously doubt that many Englishmen or other modern horsemen outside the Southwest of our own country ever used such a light hand on a bit, or wanted to. Most riders want to "feel his mouth"; and most drivers want the horse "to know what a bit is for" and want him to "take a good hold of the bit."

There is one effect of the sliding mouthpiece, invented in the days following Newcastle, which I have never seen mentioned in print; but it is very real and quite important. If a bit has a seven-inch sidepiece (a very usual length) and the mouthpiece has half an inch of play, there is quite a difference in the leverage when the mouthpiece shifts from its lowest possible position to its highest possible position. Also, if the mouthpiece is hanging as low as possible when the reins are pulled lightly, it will be acting on a lower part of the bars of the mouth—a tenderer part—than it will be acting upon when pull is increased and the bit slides up, as slide it must when pull is increased. This very action makes it difficult to adjust a curb chain so that it will give proper leverage and still not pinch the corners of the mouth. This is such a great difficulty that I never use a sliding curb, although I am quite partial to a flexible bit—one with smooth, loose juncture of mouthpiece and sidepiece.

FOUR "PROPER" BITS AT THE TURN OF THE CENTURY

By the middle of the nineteenth century, form had become so pronounced in driving, even in America, that such a detail as the proper care, and display during use, of a whiplash covers two pages of one of the leading books on driving. Bits were selected not for their suitability for a certain horse or a certain hand, but for their correctness for the particular kind of vehicle in use at a particular time of day in a particular kind of environment. It is possible to group the driving bits of the period—a period that lasted into our own century—into four general classes, each typified by a special bit. The four bits that typify the classes are called, respectively, (1) coaching, (2) Ashleigh, (3) Liverpool, and (4) Buxton.

All of them had straight bar mouthpieces. The bars were smooth on one side and corrugated on the other. Presumably the smooth side was for general use, but as all four had pivot action, the cheekpieces could be reversed so that the rough side of the mouthpiece could be used on a hard-mouthed horse. The first three bits had flat sidepieces. The coaching bit had the usual shank shaped like a 7, with two slots for reins and a loop. It had sliding action as well as pivot action and was quite flexible. The

Ashleigh also had the 7-shaped shank with slots and loop but did not have sliding action. The Liverpool had sliding action as well as pivot action, but the joints were snug and did not move as freely as the others. The bottom part of the shank was flat and provided with two rein slots. Above the top rein slot the side-piece was a circle bisected by a perpendicular bar to which the mouthpiece was attached with sliding action. On top of this circle was the ring for attachment of the bridle. The Buxton's sidepieces were made of bars of round metal. It looked much as if some enterprising bitmaker had taken a conventional four-ring riding Pelham with a very long shank, bent a large U in the lower part of the shank, flattened the U slightly, and put a slot in it. The Buxton is the only one of the four that had a bar connecting the bottom ends of the shanks.

When reins were attached to the loops in the coaching or the Ashleigh, to the top ring of the Buxton, or to the large circle of the Liverpool—which in each of them did away with the lever action—the bit was said to be used "full cheek." When the reins were attached to the top slots (the only slots in the Buxton), the bit was said to be used "half cheek." There seems to have been no special term for use of reins attached at the bottom of the shank.

To illustrate that these bits were used in accordance with the dictates of proper appointment, I quote again from a very proper book of the day, Underhill's *Driving for Pleasure*:

For single horse driving, either the Liverpool or Ashleigh is correct for all occasions, except for the show ring and park driving with ladies' traps, such as the George IV or Peters' phaeton, where the Buxton is the correct bit for single horses as well as pairs, and except also for gigs where a gig bit is correct. Gig bits, however, should not be used with other traps than gigs. For pair horse driving the Buxton is correct for the show ring and park driving and may be used for informal occasions, though personally I think it rather poor form for country driving with any kind of trap. The Buxton, however, . . . is, unless you use the "full cheek," rather a severe bit for any but a skilled driver with light hands. For pair driving a pivoted bit should always be used. The Liverpool is not so suitable for pair driving as the Ashleigh or other elbow bits, because even when the bars are pivoted they do not turn freely, so that the two inside bars are usually pulling at an angle on the bit, and do not give an even pull on the horses' mouths.

If your horse has a very light mouth, and you have not acquired very light hands, it may be better to drive with the reins in the full cheek. If, however, you have acquired light hands, the reins had better be in the half cheek of the Liverpool or Ashleigh, or in the middle bar of the Buxton, as this gives much more control and "feel" of the horse's mouth. In fact, no competent whip with light hands, particularly no woman, will want to drive a horse, however light his mouth, in the full cheek. If your horse's mouth is rather hard and there is danger of his running away, it is better to have the reins in the first hole of the bar of the Liverpool or Ashleigh, but if you drive him this way you must keep a very light hand, as it makes the pressure of the curb chain too severe, and you may make his mouth hard by a constant pressure of chain. If you are unfortunate enough to have to drive a puller, it will probably be necessary to put the reins in the second hole of the bar, and even to twist the curb chain, and to use a special form of bit with a long port or other device intended to stop a pulling horse. No woman, however, should have a pulling horse in her stable.

In pair driving the bitting is most important. It is the rarest thing in the world to find two horses who are not only well matched in appearance but have the same dispositions and require the same bitting. In fact, there is an old saying, "There is always one to a pair." By correct bitting and a proper adjustment of the coupling reins the differences in the dispositions of the two horses can be equalized, and they can be made to go well together. This is a point which is very frequently neglected by inexperienced drivers, and few coachmen really understand it, so that you must learn it yourself and see that your horses are properly bitted and coupled.

The general principle, of course, is that the slow horse of the pair should have the reins in the cheek or half cheek, while the fast horse should have them in the half cheek, or the first, or even second, hole in the bar, and it may be found necessary to put a severe bit on the fast horse and a plain bit on the slow one. Similarly, if one horse has a light mouth and the other a hard one, the bits and the coupling reins must be regulated and the curb chains adjusted accordingly. It is impossible to lay down any fixed rules to follow. It is all a matter of experiment with the particular pair of horses that you are driving.

BEARING REINS AND THEIR BITS

With the stylish carriage, gig, and trap came the bearing rein. Though it had very practical and painless uses, it soon became such an instrument of torture that laws were passed about it; but they were of little more effect than modern ones to control the setting of tails and the crippling of feet of our show horses. The bearing rein was attached either to the driving bit or to a snaffle used in addition to the driving bit. From the bit it passed, on either side, through a metal loop attached to the bridle just below the juncture of browband and crownpiece, thence through a hook on the backband of the harness.

Later, as the fast trotter, the roadster, came into vogue, the overcheck was popular, with its great variety of auxiliary bits which I shall describe later.

Another quote from *Driving for Pleasure*:

Bearing reins are required in the appointments for ladies' traps except for runabouts and pony carts, and I believe generally in their use with nearly every kind of trap, and with a single horse as well as with pairs. It is only the abuse of bearing reins, and not the use, which has led to the outcry so generally made against them by persons ignorant of the principles and practice of driving.

Bearing reins should be just tight enough to keep the horse's head up in its natural position. When so adjusted they prevent a horse from putting his head down and getting the bit in his teeth; they prevent him from putting his tongue over the bit and do a great deal toward preventing him from kicking.

Bearing reins are particularly necessary in pair driving, for however well matched two horses may be in general appearance, they seldom carry their heads naturally at just the same height. In that case the horse who naturally carries his head high should have his bearing rein quite loose and the other's quite tight, so that their heads may be at the same height. Nothing looks worse than to see two horses in a pair carrying their heads one low and one high. Most of the best authorities on driving also say, and I have no doubt that it is true, that bearing reins keep a tired horse up and make his going easy; they also keep him from nodding.

Of course, many thoughtless grooms draw the bearing reins altogether too tight, so as to force the horse's head up and make him almost ewe-necked. This naturally frets a horse, especially when he is standing still. The bearing reins should be fastened to a bridoon and not to the bit, as, if fastened to the bit, they raise it too high and are apt to spoil the "feel" of the horse's mouth.

For runabouts, at all times, bearing reins should be dispensed with, and they may be dispensed with for informal country driving in any kind of carriage, especially with a single horse. When bearing reins are used they should generally be loosened if the horses are to stand for any length of time.

The overhead check-rein should never be used, except with roadsters or trotting horses.

14. DRIVING BITS IN THE GAY NINETIES

By the end of the last century, the buggy horse and the harness race horse had come to occupy the place in our culture now occupied by the automobile. The kind of horse on which the bits just discussed were used became known as the heavy harness horse (not to be confused with the draft horse that pulled the heavy drays and farmed the land until the tractor relieved him of the job) and the buggy horse was called a harness horse, a designation also used for the horse that raced on organized tracks. The term "heavy harness horse" was used in show ring classification in all horse shows of any consequence until very recently. There was also another classification of driving horse—"*fine harness horse*"—which is still used in some shows. Such a horse was valued for his beauty and stylish action, almost as high as that of the Hackney. The fine harness horse has never been docked, as were all heavy harness horses. Instead, his artificially high, long, flowing tail was one of his distinguishing marks. There was, and still is, also the "combination horse" that was educated for use under saddle and in harness. Horse shows in many parts of the country still have classes for both three- and five-gaited combination horses.

The variety of bits used on harness horses was seemingly infinite. However, with the exception of the three-gaited combination horse in the show ring, curb bits were never used, though they remained the proper appointment on the heavy harness horse.

MOST COMMON BITS—THE BAR AND THE SNAFFLE

The workaday horse, the one that was transportation for the drummer, the doctor, the housewife, and the clerk, was most commonly driven with either one of the two types of bit. Spare bits of either or both of these two types were to be found hanging in the stables that were as common at the rear of every city lot as garages (the small private ones) were in the second quarter of this century. It was a poor home indeed that did not have a stable at the rear containing at least one driving horse.

The common types of bits were the snaffle and the bar bit. The former was never called a bridoon by harness horse people, though horsemen who used a similar bit as an auxiliary for a bearing rein always referred to it as a bridoon.

The driving snaffle used on the harness horse had a jointed mouthpiece indistinguishable from those used on running horses on the track as well as those used in a full bridle and called bridoons. However, the outward appearance of the driving snaffle was unique. Each sidepiece was attached with pivot action to the mouthpiece but without sliding action. At the bottom of the pivotal juncture of mouthpiece and circular sidepiece depended a bar two inches or more in length, round at the point of attachment and flattened and curved slightly outward toward its extremity, so that the sidepiece looked somewhat like the letter P. However, the top part of the P was circular, not D-shaped.

The shape of the sidepiece of the driving snaffle seems at first glance less practical for use on a horse guided by lateral, side-wise pulls than the egg butt, or D-shaped, sidepieces so common on running horses, and much less practical than the old full cheek snaffles, on which the sidepieces were long bars resembling those of some pre-Christian bits.

Preferable as those running-horse snaffles seem at first glance, they were impractical and had to be adapted into the harness-bit shape because many drivers attached the overcheck, always used to keep a harness horse from putting his head down, to the snaffle or bar bit, though the use of a separate, auxiliary bit for the overcheck was also common. Had the full cheek running-horse snaffle been used, without the use of an auxiliary bit for an overcheck, the overcheck would have pulled the tops of the bars of the sidepieces against the sides of the upper jaws sufficiently to cause irritation. A similar effect would have existed with the egg butt bit.

The sidepieces of the other most common driving bit, the bar bit, were exactly like those of the snaffle. The mouthpiece, of course, was not jointed. It was usually curved slightly so that pressure would come on the bars of the mouth without restricting the movement of the tongue, and it was often a more oval than round bar of iron.

While the bits just described were in the mouths of ninety per cent of the driving horses that pounded the city streets and jerked buggies over country roads, many variations of them were used by discriminating horsemen who had horses of peculiar temperament or horses that had been spoiled by previous igno-rant owners. Some of the variations, of course, were used for ostentation. Some very wise drivers, who knew the trick of "snatching back" a puller, used leather-covered or rubber-covered bars on horses that had hard mouths. The same bits were very frequently used on tender-mouthed horses and horses that had a tendency to get behind the bit. There were, and still are, listed in saddlery catalogs, bits with leather-covered and rubber-covered mouthpieces; also, bits with hard rubber mouthpieces and some with flexible leather mouthpieces. All these had side-pieces like the ordinary snaffles. On some of the leather-covered mouthpieces, the leather extended to form a round cushion or shield that came between the sidepiece ring and the corners of the mouth.

Frequently young horses, especially if they were checked very high and were ambitious, would become tender and sore at the corners of the mouth. For them these cushioned mouthpiece bits were very good. There were, and still are, separate shields of various materials and shapes to fasten on the mouthpiece just inside the cheekpiece to prevent chafing. The most common use of such shields (listed in some catalogs as "cheek guards") today is on the bits of Walking Horses in horse shows. The curb chain is usually kept long on a show-trained Walker, and he is forced to lean into the bit, either by his rider or his sore feet. This frequently causes a pinching of the corner of the mouth between mouthpiece and chain. The cheek guards prevent this.

While leather and rubber were used to prevent discomfort, countless inventions were made of pain-causing bits to control the puller, to correct the tongue loller, to straighten up the horse that had a tendency to travel diagonal to his line of progress or to hold his head sidewise, and to correct many other faults, real or imagined. It is notable that none of such driving bits (with the exception of one or two auxiliary bits for use with an over-check) employed the fulcrum and lever principle of the curb. Without exception, they employed principles of torture that date back to the days of ancient Egypt and earlier. There were mouthpieces of chain, of little balls joined by rough links, and some that resembled bicycle chain. Few of these severe mouth-pieces have survived to the present day. One of them, however, a bit formerly quite popular as a mule bit is still used to some extent on harness horses and now and then by trainers of five-gaited show horses. It has a mouthpiece of twisted wire. The double-twisted wire bit, as its name implies, had a double mouth-piece each part of which was jointed; but the joints did not coincide. This, of course, is a very mild use of the principle of the rough mouthpiece of which the ancients were so fond.

One of the most popular severe driving bits of the end of the last century and the beginning of this one was the J.I.C. bit. Its mouthpiece looked much like that of the ordinary snaffle except for a slot formed by two rods that bisected the ring to which reins are attached on the snaffle bit. The mouthpiece of the J.I.C. consisted of two rods the diameter of a lead pencil. One end of each rod was attached to the sidepiece where a snaffle is attached. The other end went through the slot on the opposite sidepiece and terminated in a loose-fitting ring to which the rein was attached. This mouthpiece had a pincherlike effect on the bars; also, it clamped the sidepieces (rings) against the outsides of the jaws.

In the last two decades of the nineteenth century and the first decade of the twentieth, several men rose to prominence because of their ability to handle horses. Their position in our culture was curious. It ranged from that of a medicine show barker almost to a position similar to that of artists like John Philip Sousa. In fact, when I was a lad I heard Sousa perform one week in the principal theater in the Midwestern city of my birth; and the next week witnessed an exhibition of horsemanship in the same theater by a man by the name of Gleason. Most of these equestrian stars, including John S. Rarey (who commanded more respect throughout America, Europe, and Czarist Russia than all others and performed in 1858 in London before more crowned heads than had ever before been assembled on English soil), had bits of their own invention, which they found more effective than all other bits. Each of such bits usually became known by the name of its inventor.

Whether the J.I.C. bit, described above, was such a bit or one named after a race horse on which it was used with success, I have never been able to learn, but it certainly got its name from one of those two sources. Another of such bits was, if my memory is correct, named after Gleason. It is now on loan to me from the bit collection of Harry Haynes, an excellent and experienced horseman of Denver and Phoenix. This bit, like the

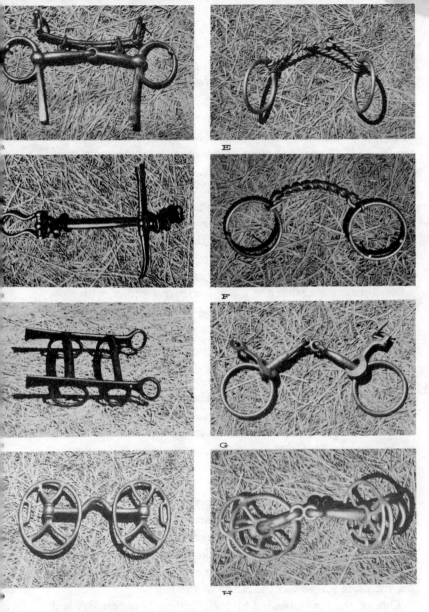

Driving and racing bits: a. Conventional snaffle with overcheck bit attached (driving and racing); b. pulley bit (harness racing); c. nineteenth century double bar harness racing bit; d. bar bit with port (driving); e. double twisted wire bit (driving); f. chain link snaffle (driving); g. Rockwell bit (driving); h. special snaffle with loose cheeks, suggestive of early Scythian bits (driving). From Harry Haynes's collection, Denver

J.I.C., was capable of causing pain on the outside of the jaws. The mouthpiece was a stiff bar, curved back on either end so that the pressure inside the mouth came well on the outside of the bars and was relatively painless to them. However, the rather intricate cheekpieces were so fashioned that rollers they contained could be made to exert severe pressure on the outside of the lower jaws.

Another bit on the same principle, one still listed in saddlery catalogs of leading firms, is the Springsteen. Each cannon of its jointed mouthpiece extends in a curve beyond the juncture of the loosely fitting ring sidepiece so that it hangs rather snugly against the outside of the lower jaw, at which point it exerts pressure when reins are pulled. The extremities of the cannons, where they press against the lower jaws, are supplied with slots so that a strap can be used under the jaw to keep the cannons tight against the outside of the lower jaw.

The only principle involved in bits of the Gay Nineties that was not anticipated by horsemen two thousand years ago is the use of the gag rein. It is in common use today on the track and on the polo field. Pulleys, rings, and slots through which round leather reins would pass freely were attached to the outer ends of the mouthpieces of either bar or snaffle bits to adapt the bit to gag action. This action was the use of pressure not against the bars of the mouth but against the corners. The pull was toward the ears rather than against the jaws. This kind of pressure was obtained by having the reins attached to the bridle at the top of the horse's head and then run through pulleys, rings, or slots at the ends of the mouthpiece. Sometimes when a gag bit was used, the horse's nose was kept down by the use of a standing martingale. However, the more a horse thrust his nose up, the more severe was the action of the gag.

One of the few bits used by both driving horse owners and on Thoroughbred race tracks, a bit still in use on the track today, is the Dexter snaffle ring bit. This has no connection with the Arabian or Moorish ring bit with its lever action, though both the Eastern bit and the Dexter are equipped with rings that go through the mouth and around the jaw.

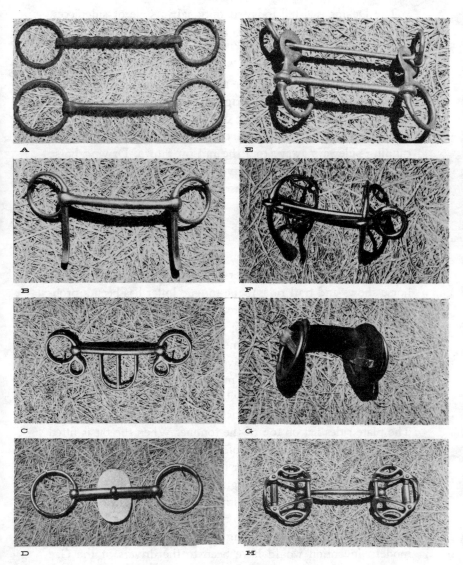

Driving bits: a. twisted bar bit and conventional bar bit; b. conventional bar driving bit, popular for a century; c. and d. special bar bits to keep tongue under bit; e. Phillips safety bit; f. J.I.C. bit; g. Stalker bit with leather covered pads and jaw strap (strap is broken); h. Gleason bit. From Harry Haynes's collection, Denver

The Dexter is listed today as optional in style of sidepieces. The "half cheek," the usual cheekpiece on snaffles, is the one used by driving horse owners. The sidepiece that is a ring only, cataloged "without half cheek," is the style seen on tracks. The large ring that goes through the mouth and under the jaw passes through a small ring that is a rigid part of each sidepiece and is located just below the juncture of jointed mouthpiece and sidepiece. On the track this is a very useful bit to keep horses from running sideways away from the rail on a turn. Driving horse owners used to claim it was very useful on a horse that shied or on one that, for any other reason, required severe pull to the side.

TONGUE CONTROLLERS

Since the days of driving horses (even in the present day of horse shows and trail rides), the tongue loller has been a problem. The horse that carries his tongue over the bit and hangs the end outside his mouth is giving evidence of human stupidity of which he is or was at some time the victim. To cure the habit, various bits have proved effective—when the original cause has been located and removed. The most common cause was, and still is, a bar bit that has attached, with a revolving joint at its center, an oval plate two and a half inches wide and four inches long. The plate rides flat on top of the tongue. When the bit is fitted very snugly up in the corners of the mouth, it is impossible for the horse to get his tongue over it. There were other similar bits for tongue lollers, some with a grill instead of the plate described above. However, it was not until recently that a device was invented to prevent as well as to cure the habit of tongue-lolling and that of hanging or lugging on the bit. What a boon that modern invention would have been to the drivers of the Gay Nineties! The device is named the Sure Win bit holder, supplied by only one horse equipment firm as far as I can determine— Miller's, 123 East 24th Street, New York City. The holder is shaped like a Y. The tail of the Y terminates in a double-sewn leather loop that lies on the horse's poll. There the crownpiece of the bridle passes through it. From that point the holder extends down the center of the horse's face to a point just below the eyes where the Y divides into arms, each terminating in a shield that fits around the mouthpiece of the bit just inside the cheekpiece. The holder can be so adjusted that it keeps the bit on the roof of the mouth.

OVERCHECK BITS

Some uses of the overcheck, by design or accident, prevented the horse's getting his tongue over the bit. The most common way of using the overcheck was to fasten it directly to the driving bit. This use, especially if the overcheck was kept tight, held the driving bit high in the corners of the mouth. Also, at such times as the driver was not pulling on the reins, it kept the driving bit up against the roof of the mouth.

While varieties of overcheck bits began to sprout around race tracks like forest mushrooms after a summer rain, horses pounding the streets and roads were driven with their overchecks attached to the driving bits or, with a few exceptions, attached to either of two kinds of auxiliary overcheck bits. The more common of these was simply a five-inch bar about three-sixteenths of an inch in diameter. It was slightly curved and was provided with a small revolving ring at either end to which the overcheck was attached. The other common kind of overcheck bit was like the one just described except that the bar was jointed in the middle.

Obviously, with either of the two popular kinds of overcheck bit, the horse usually opened his mouth, and there was considerable stretching of the corners of a horse's mouth when a continuous hard pull was maintained on the reins, as there often was because many drivers wanted a horse that "took a good hold on the reins." To keep the mouth from being pulled open and the corner of the mouth stretched between the upward pull of the overcheck and the pull on the main bit, which was downward if a running martingale was used and rearward if not, the easiest technique was to use a tight noseband. Most people wanted harness that was as simple as possible to put on, and a noseband was just one more gadget, so only the more particular person used it or any other special device to prevent stretching the mouth between bit and check.

One of the best, though least-used, devices for such prevention was a folded, double-stitched chin strap that extended up through the ends of the cannons of a specially designed bit. Obviously the horse was apt to put more pressure on such a device than he would put on an overcheck bit, so care had to be used to prevent chafing at backband or crupper.

Another device used on the track extensively and occasionally on the road was the snaffle equipped with a loop on the top of each cannon of the mouthpiece, located midway between joint and sidepiece. These loops were of the size and shape of the lip-strap loops on a modern English curb. In each loop was an oval link three-quarters of an inch long. The overcheck bit passed through these links and was thus kept from spreading the corners of the mouth more than the fraction of an inch just specified.

A similar bit was called the Philips Safety Bit. It was a bar bit with flat metal protrusions on the sidepieces above the juncture of mouthpiece and sidepiece. In each flat protrusion, one and a quarter inch above the mouthpiece was a slot through which the overcheck bit passed freely. Why the bar bit allowed more than an inch of play between main bit and overcheck bit (stiff, un-jointed overcheck bit) and the snaffle allowed a half-inch less is a mystery.

BITS FOR THE HARNESS RACE HORSE

At the close of the nineteenth century, the demand for speed in the driving horse reached the proportions of the demand for speed in automobiles in our own time. For the grand circuit of harness racing, mile tracks were built in key cities throughout the East and Midwest. The one in Columbus, Ohio, survived well into this century. As a small boy I had the thrill there of seeing Dan Patch, the fastest harness horse in the world at that time. Every county fair had its half-mile track used, with rare exceptions, exclusively for harness racing.

On the West Coast, Leland Stanford and other nationally prominent figures became vitally interested in fast harness horses. A wager between Stanford and a friend concerning what a trotter did with his feet led to the invention of the motion picture camera. Charles Marvin, Stanford's great trainer, drove each of three of Stanford's trotters one mile on the Palo Alto track in less than two minutes and eleven seconds. Bob Dobie had already driven Nancy Hanks to a high-wheeled sulky a mile in two and four-tenths minutes at the trot. John Kelly drove Directum, whose son was to break all records, to a record of two minutes five and a quarter seconds.

I neither would nor could dim the glory of the sport of kings, the running race, by comparison to the harness race. The running race as an organized sport has flourished since the day of the Duke of Newcastle, and it will undoubtedly flourish as long as there are men to gamble and horses to run. Nevertheless, there is a spark of truth in the unfair and erroneous definition of the running race as "a bunch of half broke colts ridden by midgets and scared around a fenced-in track." This definition leaves out of account such great artists as "Sunny Jim" Fitzsimmons, who in his eighth decade of life was training Thoroughbreds to gallop faster than any trotter or pacer could ever hope to travel. However, Charles Marvin and his competitors had problems that the trainers of Thoroughbreds did not have, because the harness horse is doing his thirty-mile-an-hour trip around the track at an artificial gait.

It is true that most horses have a natural trot. Even today the pace, which before the seventeenth century was a natural gait of many horses, is occasionally natural to some colts. However, the natural trot or pace is a gait not faster than the rate of ten or twelve miles per hour. When a horse without skilled training and the artificial aids of the track goes beyond that speed, he breaks into a gallop, or run.

To develop the two-minute trotter and meet the demand for speed in driving horses, much selective breeding was done. But one of the main factors in attaining the almost unbelievable speed at learned gaits was proper bitting. The fast trotter and pacer had to learn a balance that was exactly the opposite of that of the Renaissance horses of the manège. Those horses of nobility had to balance on their quarters and do all their stunts in a state of extreme collection. The trotter and pacer, on the other hand, had to reach a state of extreme extension never before achieved by a horse and impossible for any but those developed by careful and selective breeding.

The tendency of most horses when trotting or pacing beyond the limit of natural speed is to lean into the bit and bear downward on the overcheck. The steady, skilled hand on the reins keeps the gait smooth and prevents breaking. The slightest unsteadiness of the hand causes a horse to break, to grab the quarter of a forefoot with a hind foot, or to commit some more disastrous blunder.

The greater the steady hold on the reins, the greater the tendency to put the head down. Also, like any pull on a bit that puts pressure on the bars of the mouth (in contrast with an upward pull on a snaffle or gag that works only on the corners of the mouth), the pull on the driving bit tends to pull the nose in—a sure way to lose extension or even to cause collection.

OVERCHECK DEVICES

Early inventions of overcheck bits to solve the problem looked much like curb bits with bent shanks and ports upside down. The end of the shank was attached to the overcheck. This caused the port to act on the roof of the mouth. Then the port was replaced with a spoon, and a second bar mouthpiece was added, an inch or more above the first.

These bits of course caused pain. While a horse under extreme excitement and tension tends to bore into any steady pain causer, there were some horsemen who thought that such bits tended to reduce speed. So one by the name of Raymond invented what he called the Leverage Chin Check. This device used the fulcrum and lever principle, never before used on an overcheck bit. An adjustable, padded-leather nose strap was kept midway between eyes and nostrils by a strap that went up the middle of the face, between the eyes, and fastened at the poll to the crown piece of the bridle.

To each end of the nose strap was fastened a shank that curved first forward to avoid touching the driving bit and then downward to a point just in front of the mouthpiece of the driving bit. At that point it was attached to a chin strap, making the lower jaw, or chin, the fulcrum. Thence the shank curved upward to terminate in a ring for attachment of overcheck at a point several inches in front of the horse's nose and a little higher than his nostrils. The terminal rings to which the overcheck was attached were joined by a spacer or bar.

The following year a similar device was brought out by a horseman by the name of Sears. He called it the Humane Pilot. It was much simpler than the Raymond device. It consisted of a single strap of metal buttoned at either end to a nose strap located like the one in the Raymond Leverage Chin Check. From the buttons on the nose strap, the band extended toward the nostrils for a few inches then curved upward over them in an arch high enough to allow for full distention of nostrils. At a point on each side of the metal band just above the corner of the mouth, the chin strap was attached. It ran downward through a folded-leather bit guard. This passing of the chin strap through the bit guard kept the entire device in proper place on the nose. As with the Raymond Chin Check, the lower jaw acted as the fulcrum for the leverage action of the device.

The most highly praised overcheck device was one that made a horse resemble a unicorn. It was called the Governor Check. It had a metal arm five inches long extending outward from a pad on a padded nosepiece, and terminating in rings for attachment of overcheck. The latter was stiff and fitted to the shape of the nose, fastening into the cheek straps of the bridle on either side. The projecting arm was attached by a rocker joint to the nosepiece, or nose saddle, located midway between eyes and nostrils. At the joint the arm bent forward at a right angle extending toward the nostrils for a little more than an inch. Then it divided

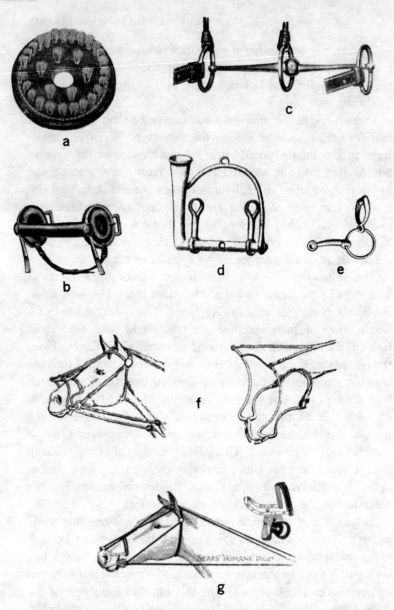

A selection of bits from the Mosemans' Illustrated Guide for Purchasers of Horse Furnishing Goods (a catalog of the 1890's) from the library of Lawrence Richardson, Scottsdale, Arizona. Many are still in use, some are unusual bits few modern horsemen have heard of. a. bit burr; b. pneumatic bit; c. regulator bit; d.

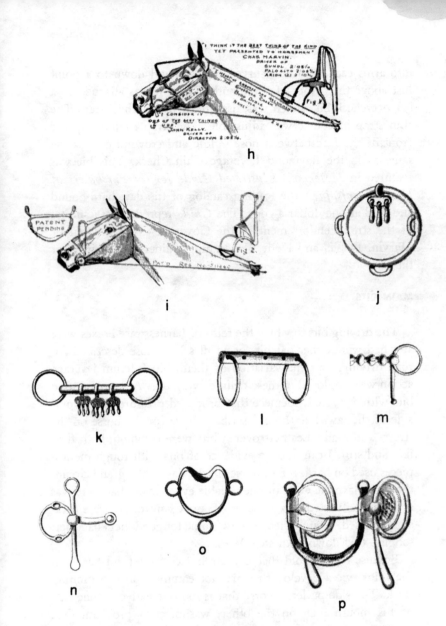

medicine bit; e. pulley bridoon; f. Raymond leverage chin check; g. Sears "humane" pilot; h. and i. the governor check (the writing is quotations from satisfied users); j. colt bit; k. mouthing bit; l. wind sucking bit; m. ball, rollers and joint bit; n. gag bit; o. rearing bit; p. humane bit with leather safes.

into arms each of which curved outward and down to a point just above the corner of the mouth. There it was attached to a bar overcheck bit, which was also attached to a chin strap. The chin strap of course was adjustable. The strap running up the front of the face between nose saddle and crownpiece was the same as in the Raymond Leverage Chin Check. This bit was featured in *Moseman's Illustrated Guide for the Purchasers of Horse Furnishings,* the leading catalog of the day, hard-bound and sold at one dollar a copy. The *Guide* reproduced facsimiles of the strong endorsement of the Governor Check written by Marvin, Dobie, and Kelly, the leading trainers and drivers of the day.

MAIN BITS

The driving bits to which the reins of harness race horses were attached were either bar bits or snaffles like those described for road driving, or some variation of them. No fulcrum leverage action was employed in these main driving bits. A few men used bits with a levered sidepiece that produced pressure on the outside of the jaw, like those described above for the horse on the streets and roads. Leather-covered bits were common, both flexible and stiff. I can find no evidence of bits with rough mouthpieces used on harness race horses in the day of the grand circuit, though I have the word of one reliable eye witness that there was at least one twisted-wire bit used. Tongue controllers were occasionally used, though then, as now, some tongue lollers had their tongues tied down with shoe laces.

Because of the hold that harness horses took (and take) on the reins, vices develop that are not common on the running track. The side puller, a horse that is more sensitive on one side of his mouth than on the other, was often a problem. One suspects that such trouble often started with a bruise from being snatched back out of a break or to lighten up a pull, or from a bad tooth. Whatever the cause, the trouble was serious and had to be reckoned with. The snaffle bit with a joint off center was frequently used to cure the habit, or to get along with it. The bit burr, to be described in connection with running horse bits, was used some but was not as practical with harness horses as with runners because the harness horse necessarily got much more daily work on a bit than did the runner and therefore the burr was more apt to produce a sore that led into worse trouble than that which it was intended to alleviate. The Regulator bit, one with mouthpiece extended beyond the sidepiece on one side, to be described in connection with the runner, was and still is used with some success in curing the side puller. At least, if it did not cure the fault, it facilitated the handling of the horse. Many side pullers tended to travel with their bodies slightly diagonal to the line of progress. With such animals the fault had to be corrected before races could be won, and sometimes the trick bits worked.

On such horses, and on those that tended to carry the head to one side, some drivers used a billiard cue extending from the body of the horse to a point well in front of his nose.

15. LATE VICTORIAN RIDING BITS

The first popular snaffle bit for riding horses was the full cheek snaffle, a bit still in use today though not nearly as popular as the egg butt snaffle or other similar bits. Tod Sloan, the farm boy from Kokomo, Indiana, the first American to overhaul an Englishman on an English track, revolutionized the style of riding of jockeys. He was the first to crawl up on a horse's withers, shorten his stirrups, and ride over a race horse's neck. This meant the end of leaning back and hanging onto a race horse's mouth. Even the steeplechase riders got forward on their horses, though they refrained, for safety's sake, from shortening their stirrups as much as did the jockeys.

All this getting forward made some change in the use of bits. With hands close to a horse's mouth so that they could direct pull up or down as needed by the individual mount, fewer martingales were used. In fact, the hand of the jockey was frequently used on the reins at about the spot that a martingale ring would be.

Gag bits and pulley bits became popular. Because of the rhythmic movement of the runner's head, overcheck bits could not be used as they were on harness horses to gain extension. Furthermore, the running horse, using a natural gait for speed, did not lean into the bit as the trotter and pacer did. Nor did the runner need the constant help of the bit to keep him in his proper gait. Though some runners had to be hand ridden for utmost speed, they did not bear downward on the bit as the harness horse did. The chief aid to extension of the runner was the forward balance of the rider, not the bit, though the gifted hand on the bit always helps a horse no matter what he is trying to do (and by the same token, the ignorant hand always hinders him!).

One of the difficulties confronting jockeys is that of keeping a horse from running wide of the rail when it is advantageous for him to keep in close. This difficulty is more common on the running horse track than on the harness track because horses used on the latter track have much longer periods of schooling to learn an artificial gait than the runners do. Therefore, the harness horse is better mannered and more amenable to his driver's wishes than the runner is to the jockey's.

To overcome this problem of running wide, the bit burr was the first device invented. It was a round leather shield that encircled the mouthpiece just inside the cheekpiece. On its inner surface were stiff bristles that stuck into the horse's cheek when the rein was pulled on the opposite side. This burr is the modern version of the old be-clawed bits of ancient horsemen. Another, later invention to solve the running out problem was the ring loosely attached to a snaffle bit. The lower jaw went through the four and a half inch ring, giving the jockey quite an advantage when he pulled sidewise. A still later invention, or group of inventions, were the Regulator bits. These bits had rigid bar mouthpieces that extended on one side several inches beyond the ring-shaped sidepiece and terminated in a ring to which the rein was attached. On some of the Regulator bits, the protruding part of the mouthpiece was telescopic so that the length could be adjusted to suit the user. Other Regulators were jointed snaffles in which the joint was not in the center. This put more pressure on the side of the longer cannon of the bit. It was especially useful on horses that were less sensitive on one side of the mouth than on the other, a problem less frequently encountered on the running track than on the harness track.

While martingales were less common after the monkey seat for jockeys became universal, as already explained, it was sometimes used, especially on less speedy tracks, to correct horses that galloped too high. The fast runner does not gallop high. This fact has had a marked effect on the newest breed of running race horses, the Quarter Horse. Breeders are developing a Quarter Horse who naturally pokes his head forward from his shoulders, not up. This has led to some sacrifice of good slope to the shoulders but makes a horse attractive to buyers. All of which reminds me of Man o' War; Mr. Riddle was able to purchase him very reasonably as a colt because the youngster looked "too much like a saddle horse to race horse buyers. His head carriage was wrong and he had big, flat knees."

How successful the use of martingales is in curing a horse that gallops too high is open to question, but it is sometimes tried. This use puts the pressure of the bit on the bars of the mouth rather than on the corners, where a snaffle usually presses, and may tend to lessen extension.

16. POLO BITS

The game of polo is ancient. We see it depicted in Chinese art centuries before Christ. It is also depicted in Persian art and that of other Oriental peoples. In the few pictures in which we can identify bits used in the game, they are those common to the country at the time. The ancients seemed to know nothing of neckrein or of the use of the lever-and-fulcrum bit as with our curbs. Today (at least until very recently) we associate the polo pony with the fast rein, the neckrein, and we find it difficult to imagine how the ancients played their ponies with lateral pull alone.

Polo was brought to the Western world by the British. In the days of the glory of the Empire, British military personnel stationed in India found the game a welcome relief from the ennui of army post life. They played on little native ponies with bits of all descriptions (except curbs) until the game became so popular that equipment began to be procured from home.

Not only did the game become so popular with British military personnel in India that they sent home for horse gear; it became so popular that they took the game home with them. This was in the days of Queen Victoria, so the full bridle was used on the ponies. And ponies they were, for the height of mounts was rigidly controlled.

The game soon came to America. The mounts were still ponies, and the game was played by imported rules. Conventions in the matter of gear were very rigid. After all, it was an English game and we had to do things in accordance with English custom. The full bridle (bit and bridoon, or in other words snaffle and curb) was the thing to use. Of course the curb had the round, straight shank with lip strap. Later the shorter shank and the sliding mouthpiece were admitted because the hard hands of some of the best players did rather horrible things to well-trained mouths. The shorter shanks gave less cruel leverage, and the sliding mouthpiece was thought (erroneously) to give some added relief. All these curbs were called Weymouths.

My memory serves to establish the approximate date of the change in rules of the game and of the advent of the tie-down (now required by rule) as accepted proper appointment for a polo pony.

At the close of the first quarter of this century, I was a young graduate assistant at Ohio State University. Since the university was a land grant school, military training was an important part of the curriculum. As part of the military facilities, there was on the campus an artillery unit, in which the most enterprising spirit was a Captain Hill. The captain let it be known in proper places that the United States Cavalry looked with favor upon the game of polo as a benefit to morale and an incentive to good horsemanship. He had arranged to have a few experienced polo mounts included with the issue of sixty-four artillery horses assigned to the unit at Ohio State, and he would be willing to organize and coach a polo team for the university if it in turn would come through with a little money from the athletic fund to provide a practice cage and defray some other expenses that were not included as items in his rule book.

A polo club was immediately organized and recognized by faculty and student body authority. However, prying loose some money from the athletic department to defray expenses of a polo team was not so easy. That department occupied the center of the stage in large universities then and continued to do so until Sputnik came along and frightened us all into giving the engineers top billing. Such an important department would not listen to the plea of any organization unless the plea had considerable prestige and support from both student body and faculty.

To gain such prestige and support, regular polo practice was started and the club combed the faculty for professors, instructors, or even assistants who would come out and join the team at practice and give the appearance of some faculty interest in the game. I was one of two who had any polo experience and a willingness to co-operate.

Such little experience as I had had prior to my practice under Captain Hill had been on ponies under 14.2 hands. Evidently the restriction on height had been raised, for some of our mounts were a little over 15 hands. Bits, however, were the conventional bit and bridoon, of English type of course. No tie-downs or running martingales were in evidence—not even a breastplate or breast collar; for though the pre-World War I, U.S. Army specifications against herring-gutted and sharp-withered horses had been changed to accommodate the Army's new enthusiasm for Thoroughbreds, our mounts—sired by Remount Thoroughbreds but out of Montana range mares—all had good barrels and needed no knots in their tails or breast collars to keep saddles from slipping back.

As the number of mounts was limited, each man was assigned one pony for practice (a situation I remedied subsequently by supplement from my own stable). I was assigned a blocky little gelding about 14.3 and was told I was Number Four. This, I was instructed by Captain Hill, meant that I was to "guard that goal, come hell or high water." There was no trading of positions, no matter where the ball went. Number Four guarded goal. Number One carried the ball. If he missed, Number Two picked it up and carried it, but only until Number One could take over again. Number Three played the field and blocked enemy attack wherever he could, passing the ball to Number One whenever he could.

Obviously such a game required horses with quick rein, perfect stop, and a get-away like a rocket. Mouths had to be light. A heavy hand was ruination to such mouths. One player who was too good with the stick to lose had a very heavy hand. The second time he came out for practice, his pony wore a bit with the shortest shank I have ever seen on a curb, and the chain was so loose that it was inoperative. I learned later that Captain Hill had quietly made the change in bit, using gear from his own private stock. I wondered at the time why a running martingale had not been added, because a curb without effective curb chain will put pressure on the corners of the mouth, like a snaffle, unless a martingale is used. Of course a curb rein run through a martingale would have outraged propriety any place at that time, but in the hunting field the snaffle rein of a full bridle was frequently run through a martingale. Had such gear been put on the mount of our heavy-handed player, not all his pull would have been on the corners of his pony's mouth, for he rode with a death grip on both reins, putting equal pressure on both bits.

My wonder about why Captain Hill had not put a martingale on the heavy-handed player's mount ended at the next practice, when I saw him explode at the mere sight of a martingale—a running martingale, at that!

To that next practice came a player, one of our best and most faithful, on his usual mount, a good little roan that did toss its head a bit as if at some previous time it had been ridden by a hand not as fine as the roan's mouth. This day that pony wore a running martingale of good English leather, finely stitched and carefully fitted to the horse. It immediately caught the eye of Captain Hill.

He roared, "What in Hell do you call that thing!"

"A running martingale, sir," meekly answered the player.

"Where did you get it?" queried the infuriated Captain.

"I bought it at J. H. and F. A. Sells Company, sir," was the reply.

There was still anger in the Captain's final word on the subject, "Dismount. Take that thing off. And lead your mount back to the picket line. If your hand is not good enough to keep that pony's head out of your face without that contraption, it is not good enough to play him."

For two years I enjoyed practice under Captain Hill and watched the Ohio State polo team develop into one that won its fair share of victories and a respected place among the extracurricular activities of the university. Then for several years I saw no more polo. In the early thirties I witnessed a game on the West Coast. Every pony was equipped with a standing martingale. I expressed my dismay to a seemingly knowledgeable spectator. He smiled at my ignorance and in a kindly way explained that no pony is now allowed on the field without a tie-down.

There are several good reasons for this change in gear. The game, once chiefly a player's sport, a means of relieving the ennui of army post routine in a foreign land, has now become a spectator's sport. It is much faster than in the old days. Height limitations on ponies is gone. The rules have been changed so that if Number Three gets the ball he assumes the duties once exclusively those of Number One. If Number Four gets the ball, Number Three may take his place and guard goal for the moment. At least so I was told by my friend watching the game in California in 1934. This change in rules makes speed a more important asset in a pony than a quick rein, fast stop, or instantaneous get-away. The race horse, the Thoroughbred, makes a better mount than the little Texas pony, the favorite of by-gone years. For many generations of selective breeding has made the Thoroughbred into a horse that knows and does one thing—*run*. He is not bred to stop or turn. When he is required to come to a dead stop from a full gallop, no moderate pull on ordinary bit and bridoon will suffice. With the severe devices necessary to stop him, or with the extreme yanks on bit and bridoon that in some instances will do the trick, he is apt to bounce so high off the ground in front that he will fall. Asked to do what he is not bred to do—stop short out of a full run—he may fight with his head and bash in the face of his rider. So, tie-downs (standing martingales) are required by official rule.

SEVERE BITTING FOR MODERN POLO

In recent years I have seen about every kind of available bit tried on polo ponies. I am glad that there are at least two exceptions—the Moorish ring bit and the old Baja California spade. However, though I have never seen either of them tried, I suspect some player irritated by the volatile temperament of his Thoroughbred has tried both of them.

Only once did I see, in the hands of a novice trainer of polo ponies, a Hanoverian roller mouth Pelham. It was gory, and the "trainer" and pony were dripping sweat.

The Hanoverian just named is a curb with a seven-inch English-type shank provided with lip strap. The juncture of mouthpiece and shank is a roller action joint, sometimes with sliding action. On each cannon of the mouthpiece are three contiguous rollers something less than an inch in diameter. At the inner terminus of each cannon the rather high port is attached by a roller action joint. These inner cannon joints are severe on the inner edge of the bars of the mouth whenever the bit is yanked sidewise. Of course, a sidewise pull also brings into play some severe action of the rollers as they drag across the bars. The bit does have a legitimate use, as I found when long ago I was at wit's end experimenting to find a solution to a problem with a spoiled horse that had a "dry mouth." However, as a means for putting a stop or a rein on a race horse for polo use, I doubt that the Hanoverian roller mouth Pelham would be very efficacious.

I have noted recently the use of various kinds of trick nosebands on polo ponies in conjunction with various kinds of curb bits. The frantic Thoroughbred, with plenty of adrenalin pumped into his blood stream from his usually abnormal adrenal glands, will yaw his mouth open at least a trifle in spite of an ordinary noseband when a curb bit is used to stop him. Any opening of the mouth seems to lessen the effectiveness of a bit, so special nosebands are used on some polo ponies. A very common kind is shaped like a figure 8. One loop of the 8 is below the bit and the other above it.

A very low noseband is apt to cut off wind, as the Greeks probably decided when they abandoned the dropped noseband of their predecessors. To guard against this, some polo players borrow a style from the harness horsemen and use a noseband that is just below the bit but provided with a strap that runs up the center of the horse's face and attaches to the crownpiece of the bridle. This strap keeps the noseband up off the nostrils. However, any noseband below the bit is bound, in my estimation, to have some effect on breathing. As the old jaquima users knew, the place for anything across a horse's nose is above the soft part of the cartilage. I suppose that the polo player trying to put a stop on a race horse is perfectly willing to sacrifice a little of the horse's breath for the sake of an advantage on the bit.

Perhaps the most effective means of stopping a race horse on the polo field is the drawrein. It is a rein attached to saddle or girth and run through the bit ring on either side. For the drawrein a snaffle or bar bit is usually used, though I saw Jim Fagan, the very competent horseman (now dead) who so successfully managed the Hearst Sunocol Ranch in California years ago, use a drawrein to solve a very common and knotty problem. Mr. Fagan and his wife, an excellent horsewoman, owned a pair (and probably several others) of beautiful parade horses, the Harvester and the Reaper. These horses had excelled in other fields but were also good parade specimens. They both had good mouths, the result of Fagan training. On several occasions I saw the Reaper ridden in a parade by an elderly gentleman whose hand was as unaccustomed to a bridle rein as mine is to a scepter. The animated horse pranced through the entire parade, each time I saw him, with neck arched at the poll and head steady. I wondered how Fagan had managed those performances. Close inspection revealed that underneath all the trappings was a drawrein of rounded leather. It fastened at the bottom of the cinch, where a tie-down fastens, passed forward between the horse's forelegs, and then ran through the rings of a curb bit! Such a rigging certainly lessened the jerks of the unsteady hand and gave the horse a little freedom for up and down movement of his head.

The drawrein on the polo field is, of course, used for another purpose—to stop and to turn a race horse. This device makes impossible the use of the neckrein, and the horse must be turned by a lateral pull, a plow rein. However, it is not unusual today to see a polo player with his reins crossed through his hand so that a twist of this wrist will give a lateral pull. This is the method necessary for the gag bit as well as for the drawrein, and both are quite common on the playing field today. A gag used in conjunction with a tie-down and a studded noseband is quite a severe piece of machinery.

One of the best devices I have ever seen for stopping a hot-headed horse that one does not have time to retrain properly was featured first in the last part of the 1920's by a Baltimore saddler. It was hailed in his catalog as a bit to cure a puller, a hard-mouthed horse. It could be used either with a single curb or as part of a double bridle. The device consisted of a special cavesson, the noseband of which replaced both the usual nose-band of a cavesson customary on a double bridle and the chin chain. Going over the nose was a double leather stitched band. This band extended from the juncture of noseband and cheek strap on one side to the juncture on the other side. To each juncture of noseband and cheek strap was attached a flat, double link chain, like a chin chain but longer. Each chain passed under the jaw and was fastened to the bit by the curb hook on the side opposite to that on which the chain was attached to the juncture. This of course made the chains from the two sides cross under the jaw, so a lip strap ring was provided on one chain.

The nose strap had three studs on the underside, so when reins were pulled, chains tightened under the jaw and pulled the studded nose strap against the nose. If "little joe" of Baltimore does not still stock this piece of equipment, any good saddler could make one.

Though I have not seen this studded cavesson with crossed chains under the jaw in use on a polo field, I am told that some polo players use such a device. One of its big advantages in the game is that it, unlike the drawrein and the gag, can be used just as easily with neckrein as can a conventional curb or full bridle.

Borrowing from his *vaquero* brother, the polo player often uses a steel cable noseband. Another such borrowing is the head chain, favorite device of some cutting horse trainers. Some trainers use a chain over the head where the crownpiece of a bridle goes. Others use it around the head above the eyes, where a browband goes. Some use it both places at the same time. Any use of the head chain, if it is attached to a stout tie-down, is an effective control and tends to lower head carriage. I witnessed the very effective use of the head chain by a trainer on one of California's most respected Arabian ranches when he needed to get an Arabian to lower its head to win a cutting horse class in a horse show—the chain being used only outside the show ring, of course; but the head was sufficiently sore for the weight of an ordinary bridle to keep it down for the short duration of a horse show class.

Whether a Thoroughbred running at full speed will stop or explode if suddenly tortured between a head chain and a severe bit is a matter to be determined by experiment, but I have seen at least one case in which the combination worked. How high the mortality rate is among players who experiment with such severe bits is a matter of interesting speculation. If Justice sleeps not, the rate is higher than that of horses on whom such experiments are tried.

The intense competition of modern polo, with its emphasis on the game and team work rather than on subtleties of horsemanship, seems to foster some uses of the bit rather shocking to some of us. Good trainers of polo ponies go the long route, teaching their mounts to respond to conventional curb and snaffle or to Pelham. Top modern trainers of polo ponies probably are more skillful than their predecessors, for the colts they handle are bred to do a job quite different from playing polo. At least the work of the modern trainer is different from that of the men who taught the Texas ponies to play and, whether greater or not, is deserving of highest respect.

17. MODERN SHOW HORSE BITS

To classify American show horses today as Eastern or Western is naïve. To use the classifications *English* and *Western* is just as bad or worse. The Tennessee Walking Horse is neither Western, Eastern, nor English. The five-gaited horse is certainly as prominent on the West Coast as elsewhere, yet he is not a Western horse. The saddle he and his brother, the Walking Horse, wear is an American invention, not English, for whoever heard of an Englishman designing a saddle to sit over a horse's kidneys! Yet such a saddle is not Western.

The classification American Show Horse under Flat Saddle is the most useful I can devise. To subdivide our field of bits for the American show horse under *flat saddle* poses another problem. Horse show classifications proliferate overnight. In the first quarter of this century, we had three-gaited, five-gaited, park hack, road hack, and hunter hack classes. When the good old plantation horse became fancy and high-priced enough, we added a class (Tennessee Walking) for him. Today we no longer have hacks. We have trail horses. What we ride in the park I do not know. The plantation horse has become the Tennessee Walking Horse and has traded his easy running walk for a sort of underslung rack that impresses the spectator and presents a problem to the rider. If John Smith is riding Alabaster Queen, we say, "John Smith aboard!" We used to say, "John Smith up," and considered seafaring phrases as very far removed from a horse show indeed. We once spoke of park seats, cross country seats, five-gaited seats, and so on. Now we speak of the saddle seat! As if some seats did not involve a saddle!

With this backward glance at the days when the public schools did not prevent every human from growing up properly, spending most of his waking hours on the back of a horse, let us proceed to a consideration of show ring bits.

THE DOUBLE BIT

The use of the snaffle and curb bits together in a horse's mouth is considerably over a century old. It is conventional to call this sort of bitting the use of a full bridle, the bit and bridoon, or the double bit. It is acceptable show ring appointment today on any three-gaited horse, including what is called in the smallest western shows the English Pleasure Horse.

The outside appearance of the curb used in such bitting must be that of the conventional English curb, that is, straight round shanks provided with loops for the lip strap, which may be either round or flat but must buckle on the near side (the rider's left side). The lip strap must pass through the special ring of the chin chain provided for it. If a chin strap is used instead of a chin chain, it should be provided with a leather loop or ring at its mid-point for the lip strap to pass through. Because maintenance of proper adjustment of curb chain or strap is very important, a chain is preferable to a strap—straps will stretch.

Some horsemen feel a chain is more severe than a strap; they use the latter. However, they might be wiser to use a chain and cover it with a leather or rubber guard. Rubber chin chain guards are listed in the catalog of one of the leading harness companies of the East Coast at sixty-five cents. The same catalog also lists a leather curb strap with never-rust link ends. The leather is of the best and least stretchable sort, doubled and double-stitched, with center lip strap ring that does not touch the horse's jaw. This is probably the best possible device for the use of the horseman who shudders at the thought of a chain under his horse's jaw.

Probably the worst possible chin chain is one that is currently very popular in the West. It is a chain made of single links. It attaches to the bit by little straps made of latigo leather, the kind of leather that stretches most. The best chain is one carried by all leading firms catering to horsemen. It is of course made of non-rusting metal, and consists of twenty-eight to thirty double links that lie flat against the jaw. The end links are single, to facilitate easy attachment to curb hooks. Care must be taken when bridling a horse wearing this or any other conventional chain to see that the links are not twisted (some "trainers" twist them deliberately to make a chain severe). This is a very simple matter. Simply take the loose end of the chain (the chain is never unfastened from the off side of the bit) in your fingers and twist it clockwise as much as possible. If it does not immediately flatten, give it a little slack, shake it lightly, and give it another twist if necessary.

CURBS FOR THE DOUBLE BRIDLE

Most current catalogs of saddlery merchants list curbs with shanks ranging from five to nine inches. Some are rigid, some have shanks that rotate at the mouthpiece joint, and some have sliding action at that joint. Mouthpieces are of great variety, with or without ports; and ports vary in size and shape. Some mouthpieces are smooth on one side and corrugated on the other, like the Liverpool harness bit. Such bits have rotating shanks, so that

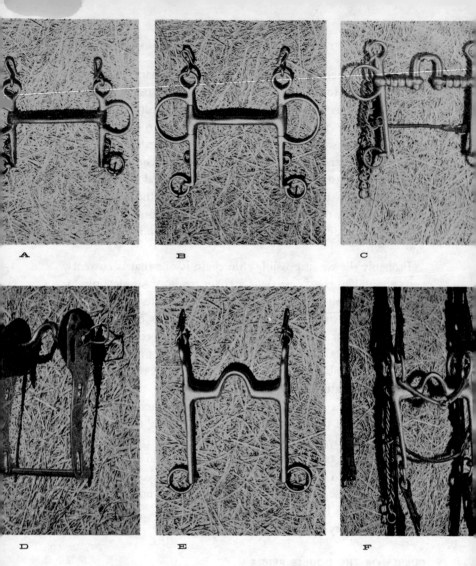

A   B   C

D   E   F

either the smooth or rough side of the mouthpiece can be used in contact with the bars of the mouth.

Two curb bits have been for many years standard equipment in the best training and show stables, each bearing the name of a horseman who rode great horses to top awards in the days when five-gaited classes lasted at least as long as forty-five minutes (the five-gaited championship at Louisville in 1915 lasted over two hours). These two are known as the Charlie Dunn and the

G

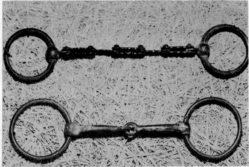

H

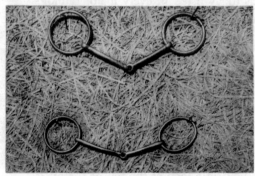

I

Riding bits: a. short swivel shanked four ring pelham; b. egg butt swivel shanked four ring pelham; c. Hanoverian roller mouth pelham; d. custom designed curb with leather guards to protect corners of the mouth; e. original Tom Bass curb; f. curb and snaffle in full bridle; g. jointed pelham; h. bicycle chain snaffle and conventional snaffle for use in double bridle; i. light snaffles for use in double bridles. From Harry Haynes's collection, Denver

Tom Bass bit, respectively. They illustrate the most useful qualities in bits for the full bridle.

The Charlie Dunn bit was designed by the horseman who, first with Ross Long and later independently, trained and rode horses to championships from the Charles Fisher stable of Kentucky, and many others. Its mouthpiece is a bar without port, slightly oval-shaped and of larger circumference than most curb mouthpieces. It is bent a trifle to allow plenty of room for the tongue. The cheeks are attached with revolving and sliding action, the latter allowing for about one-quarter of an inch of play. The bit is listed in Miller's current catalog as available with "7½ or 8 inch sliding cheeks" (shanks).

The Tom Bass bit was named after one of the most gentlemanly horsemen who ever rode into a show ring. He was also one of the most gifted. He has become almost a legend among the admirers of fine saddle horses. One story is told of how he found it difficult to exit from a championship ring in which he had ridden a mare of his training to victory. The judge, who knew Bass as did all prominent horsemen of the day, directed a steward to suggest to Bass that he give the enthusiastic, cheering audience the pleasure of seeing her rack once more around the ring. Bass touched his hat, reached forward, and slipped the bridle off the magnificent head and over his own wrist. Then the mare, under Bass's direction without bit, in a few rounds of the arena exhibited five perfect gaits to the joy of the spectators.

The bit Bass designed is today listed in every major catalog, though sometimes listed as a Weymouth, another name for all English type curbs. Miller's catalog lists it as the Tom Bass Show Bit, available with "7½ inch cheeks (shanks) and with 4½, 4¾, and 5 inch mouthpiece." The mouthpiece is slightly over three-quarters of an inch in diameter at the smoothly rounded juncture with the shank. From that juncture it tapers slightly, to a diameter of five-eighths of an inch, to round into the bottom of the port. The latter is one inch high (from top of mouthpiece to top of port) and an inch and a half wide at the bottom (inside to inside). The center of the bridle loop at the top of the bit is two inches above the center of the mouthpiece; and the center of the rein ring of the bit is four and a half inches below the center of the mouthpiece—a usual ratio for a seven and a half inch shank. The most distinctive features of this bit are the large, slightly tapered mouthpiece, the port ample for free movement of the tongue, and the smooth and curving junctures of mouthpiece with shank and with port. These features make it a bit that must be more comfortable for a horse than most curbs. I have found it to work better on more horses than any other curb. I wish that the Monte Foreman bit, the best Western curb I have ever used, had a mouthpiece and port like the Tom Bass bit.

Most catalogs list an "improvement" of the Tom Bass bit. It is exactly like the original except for the port, which is solid. Why this bit finds favor puzzles me, for the room for tongue movement afforded by the original is one of its assets. Some curbs have ports that join the mouthpiece in a sort of square shoulder that can easily bruise the inside of the bar on the side opposite the offending "shoulder" if a horse whips his head suddenly sidewise or the rider gives a lateral pull on a rein. Such bits would be better if the port were solid, but the Tom Bass bit with its rounded juncture of mouthpiece and port is preferable in its original form.

SNAFFLES FOR THE DOUBLE BRIDLE

Snaffles used in a double bridle have a sidepiece ring, flat or round, smaller than those on snaffles used alone. The mouthpiece may be of any style to suit the horseman on the particular horse he is riding. My preference is a mouthpiece similar to that of a snaffle on a driving bit, but I do not object to one of smaller diameter. The variety of cannons available in snaffles for use in double bridles is large. Some are of metal twisted, some of twisted wire, some of three-corner metal with a sharp edge bearing upon the bars of the mouth.

PELHAMS

The term "Pelham" is usually employed to designate the curb that is equipped with four rings and is never used in a double bridle. The extra pair of rings is at the ends of the mouthpiece. This permits the rider to use the bit without its level action. If the mouthpiece has no port and is shaped like a bar bit common on the harness track, the use of the top rings alone makes the bit perform exactly like a bar bit. Pelhams, like other curbs, are made with a variety of mouthpieces, with ports, without ports, smooth on one side and corrugated on the other, etc. The shanks are of all the lengths found in other curbs and are joined rigidly to the mouthpieces or with rotating or sliding action.

THE JOINTED PELHAM AND SPECIAL CASES

There is one kind of mouthpiece found in some Pelhams that is never part of a curb used in a double bridle. It is the jointed mouthpiece, which is exactly like the mouthpiece of a snaffle bit. This, of course, makes the bit perform exactly like a snaffle when top reins only are in use. However, there is one big disadvantage to this bit; it is almost impossible to adjust a curb chain or strap on it that will not pinch at times. Even if the top part of each shank is put in a vise and bent outward, a trick used on some curbs to obviate the pinching of a curb chain, the extreme flexibility of the mouthpiece allows the bit to get in a position that creates a bad pinch on the corner of the mouth between chain (or strap) and mouthpiece, with attendant tossing of the horse's head or other defensive actions that are a nuisance, to say nothing of the discomfort to the horse.

I have owned one horse and was responsible for another, both of whom were extremely high-strung and sensitive to anything suggesting force or restraint used against them, for both had been handled by the ignorant when first ridden. I tried a jaquima first on each of them, the universal remedy as far as I am concerned, for the spoiled mouth. The sensitive jaws could not tolerate rawhide. A cotton rope hackamore was so indefinite that they could "get no message" when I used that. I tried a bar bit covered with well-soaked leather. One tossed her head so continually with it that I could not get her attention for any kind of communication. The other kept his nose out with it so that any signal of pressure I used pulled on the corners of his mouth and made him respond by yawing his mouth open and giving continual short thrusts with his nose. A noseband was a signal for a fight, which was the last thing I wanted with that overbred hothead. I tried a snaffle covered like the bar. Same result with both horses, though less violent. Next, I tried the snaffle with a running martingale. The head tosser described a lower arc with her head and added a side-to-side whip to her repertory. The other put his heart and soul into a fight to get his head up.

Finally, I tried a jointed Pelham, using leather guards around the mouthpiece just inside the cheekpieces to avoid pinching the corners of the mouth. That worked like a charm, a cautiously employed charm. So again I had brought home to me the fact with which I have so often been impressed, that while a good horseman rarely needs more bits than those in a full bridle, each bit in the catalog has its special virtue and there are rare cases in which one special bit is the only one just right. In the two cases just described, the jointed mouth Pelham *with guards* was the one just right. Had I omitted the guards or used the chain (I used a rubber guard with it) a trifle too tight or too loose, I'm sure that bit would not have worked.

THE WALKING HORSE BIT

Another curb bit prominent in American show rings since the Tennessee Walker's major role has become that of spectacular showpiece instead of delightful mount for an owner, is the Walking Horse bit. In a magazine article in the late 1930's Burt Hunter, who with the help of a very few other Tennesseeans set up the stud book for the breed of horses formerly known as the Plantation Horse and organized an association for its promotion, described the bit appropriate for the Tennessee Walking Horse. Such has been the proper appointment for the Walker ever since. There is one variation in the shanks (cheeks) allowable: they may be either rigidly attached to the mouthpiece, as described by Hunter, or they may be attached by a sliding action joint. The eight or eight and a half inch (optional) shank is straight from juncture of mouthpiece to bridle attachment. From juncture down, the shank is S-shaped and slopes rearward, so that a straight line drawn from juncture to rein ring (loosely jointed) would be at a 45-degree angle with the part of the shank above the juncture. This angle is very important, because the show ring Walker works òn the bit at all times (sometimes ahead of the bit); and when his head is set in the approved style, there is very little leverage action. However, should he poke his nose out, an eight and a half inch shank on such a bit would give a very severe leverage. To increase this difference in leverage action when the head is set and when it is not, many Walking Horse showmen use a very long curb strap or chain and prevent the pinching of the corners of the mouth that a too-long chain normally creates, by using bit guards just inside the shanks at the corners of the mouth. This long chin strap decidedly increases leverage when the horse's nose is thrust forward (a rarity in a Walker).

This bit and the special way of using it prompted a serious discussion with political overtones recently. Some excellent horsemen friends of mine who have strong Republican sympathies and little knowledge of Walking Horses confronted me with a cover on *Life* magazine portraying President Johnson riding a Tennessee Walking Horse. He was sitting like an old-time rider of a Plantation Horse—feet slightly forward and relaxed in the saddle. He was holding his reins in two hands wide apart and quite evidently was having to exercise a little skill to steady the walk at the exact moment the picture was snapped.

"How do you like having that kind of a horseman for your President?" they queried with a kindly chuckle.

"Well, he looks to me as if he is doing a pretty good job of riding a Walker. They are trained to guide like plow horses and to lean into the bit. Sometimes they tend toward a pace and the side swing of the head has to be stopped to hold them to the walk, which accounts for the momentary position of the hands, if that is what seems funny to you," I answered, a trifle on the peevish side.

"But look at that business suit he is wearing," my friends countered, now quite amused at getting under my skin.

This conversation took place in my study (what the old-fashioned call my den) and I happened to have at hand for reference a copy of the November 1939 issue of *The National Horseman* magazine. The cover picture on that magazine, somewhat battered by the years I have treasured it, is a colored picture of Mr. and Mrs. E. E. Chapman's Sir Charles Allen, 350097, one of the leading stars of the tanbark in 1939. The rider is wearing a business suit. I displayed the magazine with no comment.

The cover picture on that issue of *Life* did not reveal the kind of mouthpiece built into the bit the President was using, but it is safe to assume it was one shaped like that commonly used in a bar bit for a driving horse, or it had the port usual in Weymouth bits, or it had the extra-wide, low port now becoming popular with Walking Horse trainers. Any one of such mouthpieces are available in Walking Horse bits and are correct appointment.

MODERN BITS FOR THE HUNTER AND JUMPER

Any statement about the "correct" bit for the hunter and jumper, if noticed by devotees of such horses, will arouse strong protest and criticism. It is safe to say that the curb (Weymouth or any other) with only one pair of reins is decidedly *not* the proper bit for the hunter or jumper. Even the four-ring Pelham is frowned upon by some devotees, especially those who prefer the snaffle, with or without two pairs of reins (one going through a running martingale). Any bit that tends to make the horse hesitant about fully extending himself is certainly not a good one for the hunter, or for the show jumper, either, though he only fully extends on the approach to some jumps.

For many years it has been quite permissible to appear in the hunting field or on a jumper in a horse show using a full bridle, a bit and bridoon, or a double bridle. It has been many years since I have seen a full cheek snaffle in such places, but I suspect it would not be the object of much ridicule today, and it certainly is an ideal bit on some hunters now as it was in the days of the Duke of Newcastle.

One of the best bits to use on a hunter or jumper with perfect mouth and manners is a big-ringed, flat-ringed bridoon with a mouthpiece of ample diameter. If the horse has a slight tendency to poke his nose out at the wrong time, or if the rider wants to

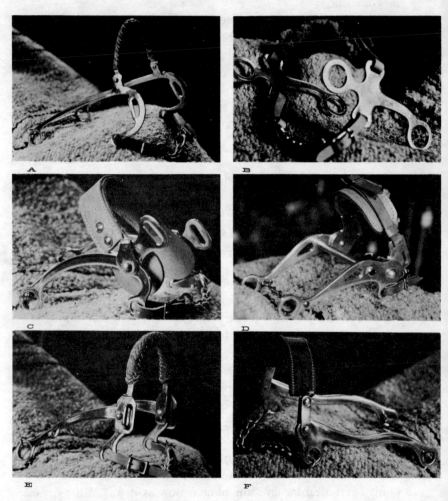

a. Hackamore bit with leather-covered cable nosepiece; b. T-shaped hackamore bit; c. Hackamore bit with leather guard to prevent chafing; d. Hackamore bit provided with mouthpiece; e. Hackamore bit with braided leather noseband, steel center; f. Hackamore bit with leather-covered flat metal nosepiece, a local favorite. From *Out of the West*, Louis Taylor, A. S. Barnes and Company be sure he can avoid pressure on the corners of his horse's mouth whenever he wants to, he may use such a bit with two pairs of reins, one going through a martingale.

At the last show I witnessed in Phoenix, Arizona, in which California horses took most of the trophies, I saw on two different jumpers a patented hackamore, or hackamore bit. How this is regarded by the custodians of propriety, I am not sure; but the horses performed perfectly in that gear, and they were competing in performance classes.

As I mentioned earlier in this book, the protection of a hunter's mouth against an inept hand is often a very important matter, sometimes a matter of life and death taking precedence over considerations of etiquette. A well-constructed hackamore bit, one that has nothing going through the horse's mouth, is a good defense.

18. DRAFT HORSE AND SPECIAL BITS

The earliest record of a draft horse bit I can find is a medieval tapestry that depicts a horse pulling a harrow in the garden of a monastery. He is wearing a curb bit apparently shaped, on the outside at least, somewhat like a modern Weymouth curb. The earliest bits used on the heavy horses of English coaches, as far as can be determined, were curb bits. The shanks or cheekpieces were elbow-shaped or 7-shaped.

Pastoral scenes by Rubens and other painters in the seventeenth century depict work horses wearing bits that do not have leverage. Possibly rural poverty, in contrast to the affluence of the carriage folk of the cities, caused the use of the simplest of bits.

The machine age brought with it the demand for power in the collar. All breeds of horses carrying a heavy percentage of the Great Horse of olden times grew in value. The best large

156

breeding stock from the French region of La Perche, and from Scotland, England, and Belgium were sought out by American importers. When the progeny of this stock was used on farms to pull the agricultural machinery, straight bar bits or snaffles were used. The most careful users chose bits with mouthpieces made of bars or cannons quite large in diameter, for on a heavy pull most drivers liked to take a good hold of the reins to keep the team together and at a slow, steady walk. With such a heavy use of the reins, a large diameter of mouthpiece was much more comfortable in the horse's mouth than one of small diameter. Of course some drivers on some horses used less comfortable bits—double-twisted wire ones, for example; but the leverage bit, the curb, was practically unknown on the horses that tilled the soil. Even the horses used on the heavy drays in the cities were driven with bar bits or snaffles. The only use of curbs on heavy draft horses was seen in the fancy draft horse hitches displayed at horse shows.

At the turn of the present century a Dr. Hartman, who amassed a fortune by his manufacture of Perunia, a patented tonic antedating Geritol by three-quarters of a century, raised on his 7,000-acre farm in Ohio's Scioto Valley great Norman horses from stock especially imported from France. When a very little boy I once saw ten Hartman farm mares hitched to a Peruna wagon driven down High Street in Columbus, Ohio. Each of those mares probably weighed close to a ton (a tremendous size at that time). People on the sidewalk stopped to admire, and all traffic was at a standstill. I still recall the big burnished nickel rings on the snaffle bits on those mares!

Horses and mules pulled the great freight wagons of the West, where on saddle animals the curb and the spade were the only bits in use. However, the mules and horses that pulled the freight and those that pulled the heavy combines in the great wheatlands of the Northwest never wore curb bits. The big teams, sometimes comprising more than twenty animals, were handled by a jerk line, a technique that merits a book exclusively devoted to it, if there is an articulate horseman still alive who really knows it. The jerk line was attached to only one of the leaders, intelligent horses trained to a perfection that would put to shame our five-gaited champions. Those leaders wore snaffle or bar bits.

The stagecoach teams, of four, six, or eight horses, were driven with a pair of lines for each pair of horses. What a handful some of those drivers had! They negotiated the tortuous, narrow mountain roads with snaffle or bar bits, often using half-broken horses for wheelers or swing team. It is stoutly maintained by eyewitnesses that the best of those drivers could direct a team around a hairpin turn by a handful of lines and at the same time flick a fly off the nigh leader's ear without touching a hair.

When Henry Ford started to make tractors, draft horse breeders, who were a very important part of our economy at that time, became concerned. Leaders in organizations devoted to individual breeds got behind the American Horse and Mule Breeders Association. They hired a paid secretary, the most competent and intelligent horseman available, Wayne Dinsmore. Dinsmore directed research in the raising, feeding, and using of horses to develop ways of making the horse such an economical source of power that no tractor could compete with him.

One of the techniques developed by Dinsmore was a way of using a multiple hitch of horses that could be expanded to any size to meet the power requirement of the most modern farm machinery. Multiple hitches had of course been in use, but they required some special skill on the part of the driver and usually some special equipment. The hitch that Dinsmore developed could be handled by any farm boy who could drive a gentle team, and in those days most farm boys could. The "eveners," which ensured that each horse pull his share and only his share of the load, could be made by anyone who had a saw and a brace and bit.

Each horse of the multiple hitch wore a bar or snaffle bit, but the two lines the driver held in his hands went only to the bits on the lead team. Each horse except those in the lead team was kept from getting too far ahead by a Y-shaped buck line. The tail of the Y was attached to the draw chain. The arms of the Y went through the hame rings and then to the bit. To keep the horse in line, so he would not pull out sidewise or lag too far behind, he was attached by a strap on his bit or a stout neckrope run through the bit ring to the singletree of the horse ahead of him.

The method Dinsmore advocated for using three or four horses abreast was not new. I had used it on my grandfather's farm long before Dinsmore became the champion of the cause of the draft horse. However, it was not widely used or understood until Dinsmore with his wide mailing list and excellent pamphleteering spread the gospel.

One rein of the three- or four-horse hitch went to the outside bit ring of each outside horse. Each of these reins had attached to it about two feet behind its passage through the hame ring a check rein like an extended arm of a Y. This check rein, like the ones on every two-horse team harness, went through the inside hame ring of the outside horse and then to the bit ring of his mate. The inside bit-ring of the outside horse was attached by a strap, adjusted to proper length, to the inside hame ring of his mate. In a four-horse team, the inside bit ring of each inside horse was attached by a properly adjusted strap to the inside hame ring of his mate. All lines and straps were attached to bits by snaps. The properly adjusted straps on the hame rings were not removed from the hames when teams were unhitched—just unsnapped from the bit.

With multiple hitches for plowing, the most foolproof method was to string the teams out in pairs, so that one horse of each pair walked in the furrow. For disking and other work not involving a furrow, the lead team was often composed of three horses. The teams between the leaders and the machine or wagon were, with the convenient Dinsmore hitch, always worked in pairs, each horse bucked back to the draw chain and tied in front to the singletree of the horse ahead of him.

This technique did much to lower the cost of the use of horses for farm power, for it could be used by ordinary farm labor that would quickly put a tractor out of commission. Even today, when the tractor has completely vanquished the horse as a power source, there is a large dairy farm in Maricopa County, Arizona, bordering an Indian reservation, on which the most readily available help gets along well with horses though they would quickly wreck tractors. On this farm are some two dozen or more of the finest Suffolk Punch horses to be found on this side of the Atlantic—and not a single tractor! This dairy farm is an odd contrast to most farms throughout the land, where every farm boy or hired hand can operate a tractor with reasonable safety to it and himself, but few of such boys and fewer still of the hands can replace a bit in a bridle and adjust it properly. This explains why a worn-out gentle team will go at auction for an astonishingly good price, while fine young Percherons, Shires, and Clydesdales unused to a bit are rounded up, loaded on box cars, and sent to the canneries.

BITS FOR SPECIAL USES

For centuries, man's inventiveness that was focused on bits resulted in novel ways to cause pain to horses. Only in the last century did it seem to occur to the human mind that the bit could serve other useful purposes.

In the catalog of C. M. Moseman and Brother was listed a "Medicine Bit." It consisted of an L-shaped metal tube closed at the lower end of the L and expanding slightly into a funnel at the other. The lower arm of the L served as the mouthpiece of the bit and was loosely encircled by two metal pieces from which short arms extended terminating in loops for the attachment of bridle cheek straps. In the center of the mouthpiece was a hole to permit medicine to run slowly out of the hollow mouthpiece onto the horse's tongue. The funnel part of the bit was kept upright by a small rod that was attached to the funnel near its top, and went over the horse's nose and down to the end of the mouthpiece on the side opposite the funnel. At the center of the large loop that the rod described over the nose was a ring to which a strap or rope could be attached, the other end of which went up the center of the horse's face and attached to the crownpiece of his bridle.

One wonders what lethal potions were poured down such funnels by home remedy enthusiasts. Undoubtedly, some of the medicines administered via the medicine bit were beneficent, like the old favorite, Spohn's, which may have no curative properties but certainly gives temporary relief to some irritations of the upper respiratory tract. Whether the sum total of human home remedies administered to horses has added to or diminished equine mortality is a moot question. However, the medicine bit may have lessened one common kind of fatal suffering horses have experienced ever since man learned to use a drenching bottle, a common cause of fatal equine pneumonia. One of the most gruesome treatments of a horse I have heard of for some time would have been avoided, perhaps, if the medicine bit were still popular.

Here is the story of the treatment as related to me recently by a very competent veterinarian:

When the doctor arrived at a stable in response to a call, he found a horse prone and suffering from severe shock. Its respiration was labored and the stethoscope revealed fluid in the lungs.

The owner's recital of the case went like this:

"Yeah, Doc, he had a hell of a case of colic, so I caught him as soon as I could when he laid down and held his nose in the air and poured Alka-Seltzer down it. Thought that would be a good idear because I seen you put worm medicine down his nose with a rubber hose."

"Well," replied the more honest than diplomatic doctor, "I can cure his colic, but the Alka-Seltzer you gave him went to his lungs and he will die of foreign body pneumonia."

"Oh, hell, Doc, he snorted all that Alka-Seltzer out of his nose. Just cure the colic and he'll be all right," was the optimistic response.

So one more horse had to suffer man-made misery as he readied himself for his last useful function, performed in the fertilizer works the next day. Perhaps had the Alka-Seltzer been administered by a medicine bit, it would have fizzed harmlessly onto his tongue and out of his mouth and he could have served his master, one of the higher animals, for many more days.

Another special purpose bit listed in Moseman's catalog as a Windsucker bit is, I have been told, still used now and then today. It is simply a pipe through which five holes have been drilled. Two of them near the ends of the pipe hold the bridle rings, and the three others are spaced equidistantly. How successful the bit is in curing windsuckers, if that is its purpose, I have never been able to learn. The only remedy I have seen used with any success is the cribbing strap. It does not cure anything, but it prevents cribbing or windsucking; and I have known show horses that were confirmed cribbers whose trainers used cribbing straps on them and kept them in top shape and winning their share of ribbons.

Even John S. Rarey, the most highly gifted horseman about whom I have ever been able to gather any substantial information, used a special purpose bit. It was one provided with an enormous wooden mouthpiece, a simple, straight bar. Rarey said that a muzzle on a biting horse does not cure him; it only prevents his biting while he is wearing it. The wooden bit, Rarey said, would cure the vice if properly used. He told of a zebra brought before him as an untameable biter, during one of his tours through the Near East. When the animal found it could not bite and that Rarey treated it with kindness and complete confidence, rubbing it behind its ears and stroking its neck, the animal by degrees abandoned its vice. Rarey used the wooden bit on Stafford, a horse with a reputation for viciousness, the first time he drove him. It is a good bit to use on any colt while he is being harnessed or groomed, said Rarey, if the colt has a tendency to crib bite at such times.

I have often wondered exactly what kind of bit Rarey used on the team of bull elks he drove, when a teenage boy, to a light runabout at the head of the Fourth of July parade in Circleville, Ohio, witnessed by my grandparents and other reliable people whom I have questioned. They all said he drove the team quietly with bits, apparently simple driving bits, which would mean snaffles or bars. However, I suspect that Rarey had a special elk bit that has as yet never come to light.

 ## 19. FRONTIER BITS AND MODERN VARIATIONS

The spade and the ring bit were described earlier in this book in connection with history of the use of bits in the Near East and North Africa. The origin of the spade is today usually credited to the Moors, though I suspect they borrowed the principle and worked out their own significant design on the cheekpieces. The ring bit first appearing on this continent has no connection either in origin or mechanical principle with the ring bit used on race horses, described in connection with my discussion of bits used to correct "running out" on the race track.

Whoever invented the ring bit, the spade, and the jaquima, it was the Moors who took them to Spain. The conquistadores took them to the New World, along with Christianity, which enabled them to "reduce" the Indians, as the good padres termed their exploitation. The early method of using the jaquima (hackamore) and the spade is accurately and charmingly described by Tom Lea in *The Hands of Cantu*. In my *Out of the West* I have given a less charming but more detailed description of it. The jaquima was used on the colt first, and the use was continued until the young horse was thoroughly responsive to the neckrein and, as Henry Wynmalen so aptly puts it, "accepted the bit." That is, until the slightest change in the slack reins would be responded to by flexion at the poll and a touch of a rein on the side of the neck would be responded to by a turn on the hindquarters.

Those early rawhide hackamores of Baja California were not the huge things now popular. The rounded loop over the nose was about twice as large in diameter as the V-shaped part ending in a round knot under the chin. The shanks of the V were often braided square or six-sided, and the buttons that kept the cheekpieces forward so that they came down the cheeks just behind the eyes were the same diameter as the nosepiece.

The shanks under the jaw carried the "authority" of the hackamore in the hands of those Spaniards. On a less sensitive young horse the rawhide often removed some hair before he was familiar with the "language" carried by the reins. Sometimes even a bit of hide went with the hair. But the green horse soon began trying to get along with his rider and to figure out what the reins were saying.

During most of the training with the hackamore, the spade, unused, hung in his mouth. By the time the rider began to vary the slack of the spade, the horse was working in response to variations of the slack in the rein of the hackamore and to the light swing of it toward his neck for a turn. The rawhide reins attached to the bit by a short length of light chain had a little more weight than our leather reins. Also they were provided with buttons, two or more spaced closely together on each side right where the rein would touch the neck as signal for turning. Those reins of the spade were held in the lightest of hands; and it was the swing of the slack rather than shift of tension that communicated.

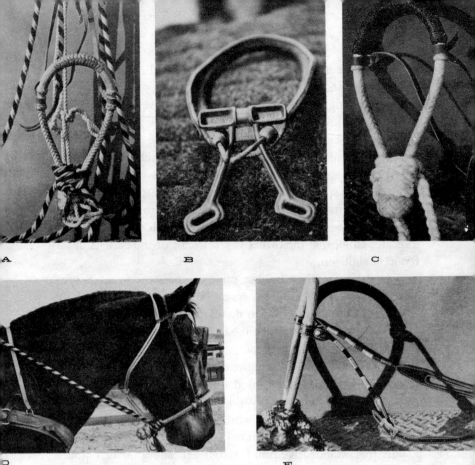

a. bosal with fiador; b. patented "Easy Stop," a device to stop horse quickly by causing intense pain, fortunately rapidly falling out of favor; c. bosal with white nylon reins (no tie rope) for exhibition use; d. properly adjusted bosal with fiador; e. bosal with split-ear headstall, for show ring use. From *Out of the West,* Louis Taylor, A. S. Barnes and Company

I once asked a friend of mine riding a beautifully trained horse with a loose-jawed spade, "Would you let anyone else ride that horse with that bit in its mouth?"

"Yes," was his reply, "if I first unsnapped the chains from the bit and then tied them to it with light cotton wrapping string."

The spoon of a spade can do a considerable amount of damage

to a horse's mouth if it is used with a lateral pull, which is never necessary on a horse with a good rein. The spoon not only keeps the horse's tongue where it belongs, it also gives him a chance to "talk" to the rider by the slightest use of his jaw muscles—a sort of "feed-back mechanism," to attempt the phraseology of modern computer specialists. However, such subtleties are lost on all but those who spend most of their lives with horses and habitually use spades; and the spade is as out of place in a smart modern tack room as a tomahawk in a modern arsenal, and a good deal more dangerous. To find one in such a place possibly indicates either that the owner is a collector of the curious or an ignorant show-off.

When the American cowboy came on the scene in the South-west, he frequently used the spade bit. His job in those early days was to do what he had to do with half-wild cattle built for speed, and do it much of the time from the back of a half-broken cayuse. Careful training of mounts was nonexistent. There was little time for it; furthermore the dangerous work and the thiev-ing by Indians and whites caused a high replacement rate for the *remuda*. Horses were cheap. Wild ones could be caught and used until crippled by the rough work or stolen because they were good at it. What a cowboy wanted for his work with a horse was "spurs that would drive him through hell and a bit that would stop a locomotive." He put rowels in the spoon of his curb bit. Occasionally he would use a ring bit, for that would turn even the most contrary critter, by a plowline yank. The ring kept the contraption from pulling sidewise through a horse's mouth. This last-named virtue of the ring bit made it useful on mules and burros, though the latter seldom wore bits of any kind.

As mentioned earlier in this book, this bit is still a favorite in localities where Basque herders are the best available help. Why these people from southern France prefer the bit is a mystery.

Another mystery is one possibly explainable by reference to the poverty of exploited natives or by close scrutiny of the man-ner in which Spanish influence spread on this continent; it is the difference in the use of the hackamore in North and South America.

The Gauchos of the Argentine used a sort of hackamore that did not act on the jaw. Its authority lay in its effect on the soft part of the nose. It was very loose and suspended just above or across the nostrils by a crossed pair of straps running up the face and attached to the top of the headstall at the base of the ears. This was not a training device leading up to the use of a bit but the everyday, working gear of the Gaucho, who even today frequently uses it as work gear without bit.

Such "bitless bridles," says Margaret Cabell Self in her *Horseman's Encyclopedia,* are typical of Arabia, also.

Though the spade and the ring bit seem the most remarkable of the bits of the early frontier, they were certainly not the only ones. The half-breed was probably so-called because its port was not as high as the spoon of a spade but considerably more than that of a curb, and also because the high, narrow port of the half-breed always contained a "cricket," usually a roller or several small rollers. There were no braces on the half-breed, so its contact with the bars of the mouth was higher than that of the spade, which was kept below the corners of the mouth by the brace that ran from high on the spoon to the cheekpiece. The cricket, whether in spade or half-breed, was usually of copper— always of copper if the bit was made south of the border. A firm and widespread belief still held in the back country of the Southwest and south of the border is that copper has a quieting effect on a horse's nerves. Every handmade bit I have ever bought in Mexico, and I have quite an assortment of them, has some copper comprising at least part of the mouthpiece. Sometimes there are thin and innocuous rollers around the mouthpiece either side of the port. Always copper comprises the cricket, which may be nothing more than two or three little strips of copper suspended from a tiny rod running crosswise in the port; or, again, it may be a unique and ingenious arrangement of keys, like those in an English mouthing bit.

It was from Mexico that the greatest variety of bits came when the West was young. Those early bitmakers were artists. All of their decorations on the shanks were suggestive of Oriental symbols, though I have never seen on any of them any part of the human body portrayed, as one was on ancient Persian bits, for instance, to symbolize masculinity or fertility. On the northern side of the border, less Oriental, less subtle art was displayed by bitmakers. They made curbs, half-breeds, and even a few spades with shanks in the shape of pistols or of a girl's legs.

Most of the bits of the Southwestern frontier were handmade, and many of them came across the border, though the Mexican bits made for the starved ponies of Sonora and other northern Mexican provinces were so small that they often had mouthpieces too narrow even for the little cayuses of Texas and California cowboys.

The Mexican bits became known by the geographic names of the area in which they were made. The Hermosillo bit, for instance, is still well known among men who actually use horses today on their cattle ranches. The Hermosillo bit has all the features most liked in a bit by range folk of the early days and of today. The juncture of mouthpiece and sidepiece was loose and flexible but artfully contrived to make pinching impossible. The leverage of the shank was about like that on a seven-inch English Weymouth, but the shank from mouthpiece down was curved. The curve has two advantages. First, because the Western saddle of frontier days made the rider hold his hand high, a straight shank lost most of its leverage, while a backward curve of the shank retained the leverage though the pull on the bit was upward. Second, when a horse was "ground tied" while his rider was dismounted to mend barbed wire (pronounced *bobbed war*) or examine an injured calf, the horse could graze without having the bit jab at the corners of his mouth, as a straight-shanked curb would.

The Hermosillo's port was fairly high and wide enough to discourage putting the tongue over the bit. Inside the port was a little rod on which rolled loosely a copper cricket.

Many good Western horsemen believe, and I concur, that a high-mettled horse likes a loose bit and a cricket because he enjoys having something to play with—a very different equine occupation from the champing at the painful bit or checkrein often seen in Eastern horses ridden or driven on a tight rein.

Those ponies of the days when the West was young often had tongues that were almost severed by rough handling on a spade or a draw rein on their first saddle. So many a cowboy would work the mouthpiece of his bit over whenever he could get near a forge. He would make the port high, wide, and smooth, with no corners where the port turned upward from the mouthpiece. Even today there are left a few cowboys of the old stamp. They are, above all else, individualists. Almost any one of them will shamefacedly admit that the first thing he does with a new piece of equipment, no matter what it has cost him out of his tiny paycheck, is to "work it over a little" when he gets back to the ranch. If it is a bit, he takes it to the forge on a Sunday when nobody is using the anvil. If it is something made of leather, he borrows a leather punch and takes out his pocket knife. So the varieties of mouthpieces and of shanks of those early Western bits is almost equal to the number of cowboys working the ranges. The one thing they all had in common was that they were all leverage bits employing the principle of the fulcrum and lever. Only recently has the snaffle become a favorite training bit for the Western horseman, who now often prefers it to a hackamore on a colt.

CAVALRY INFLUENCE AND COLD BLOOD

While Spanish influence in bits and their use spread north to the Canadian border, as is so faithfully illustrated in the work of Charles Russell, the spade and the half-breed bits were less common than those that revealed the influence of cavalry gear—and some that were inventions peculiar to the Northwest, such as the curb with a large ring for a lower shank. This was a bit that got down into Texas, probably brought back by cowboys who had been north on a cattle drive. In addition to the influence of the United States Cavalry, another factor contributed to the difference in bits north and south. It was the greater and earlier infiltration of cold blood, draft blood, in the horses of the Northwest. Bits of the Northwest were, very generally speaking, larger and coarser than those of the Southwest. Sidepieces of the silver-mounted bits of Mexico were often flat pieces of metal, while the shanks of the Northwestern bits were of round metal.

One of the cavalry bits used in early Indian warfare of the West became very popular in the Northwest. It survived as a cavalry bit until the day Teddy Roosevelt led his charge up San Juan Hill and is to be seen on the statue of Bucky O'Neil, which commands the courthouse square in Prescott, Arizona.

This bit, which lasted so long with so few variations, had a shank that was about eight inches long. The top ring was quite large or double, so that pinching of the corner of a horse's mouth between lip strap and mouthpiece was minimized. The lower part of the shank was decidedly S-shaped and almost impossible to lip. The S did not slope back like a Walking Horse bit, so its leverage was quite powerful, powerful enough to make a strong impression on a big, cold-blooded jaw.

U.S. cavalry bit of Spanish War days. Bucky O'Neill's statue, Prescott, Arizona

A few years ago I wanted one of those old bits and searched long in vain. Finally I found in a little saddle shop a new bit that was an exact replica of the old cavalry one except that an "improvement" had been made in the mouthpiece. It had the fairly large diameter, the rounded upward curve of the comfortable, wide, and fairly high port, but it was covered with copper. Evidently the maker or the horseman who ordered the bit adhered to the old belief that copper, or at least the taste of it, has a quieting effect upon a horse.

20. MODERN WESTERN BITS

Most of the bits seen today at rodeos and in Western classes in horse shows are of designs based upon the bits of the frontier. One of them is a combination of details from bits of the Old West and one frequently used in Virginia and Kentucky at the beginning of this century. Today in the West it is usually called a colt bit. It has a jointed mouthpiece like a snaffle, attached to seven and a half inch curb sidepieces, like the old Southern bits, on which the shanks were straight and so necessarily equipped with lip-strap loops. However, the modern Western version has shanks that are curved backward an inch or so below the juncture of the mouthpiece like a slightly bent elbow, and they have no lip-strap loops.

One Western bit extremely popular today is based on the old

half-breed but has a distinctive innovation of detail. The port, much lower and broader than that of the old half-breeds, still contains a copper roller (cricket) but a copper hood, the innovation, smoothly spreads from side to side of the base of the port and up to the top of the port, rounding out over it to give free play to the cricket, which is in contact with the tongue. I am at a complete loss as to the advantage of the bit that makes it so popular. The shanks are of round metal curved backward like a grazing bit, about seven inches long. They are joined to the mouthpiece by comfortable, smooth, loose joints, like those common to many Southwestern bits of the old days; and the lower ends of the shanks are connected (so they cannot be spread apart by a lateral pull on the reins) by a bar of small diameter loosely jointed to the bit rings. This feature like the jointed mouthpiece is not new and so cannot account for the bit's popularity. I have asked many horsemen who use the bit why they prefer it, but the answers I get have no common denominator with which I can explain the bit's appeal.

Perhaps the most obvious difference between the old and the new in Western bits, especially in the Southwest, is the decrease in the number of flat shanks. Shanks are now mostly made of round metal.

There are two notable exceptions among low-priced, mass-produced bits. One is a spade with shanks shaped exactly like an old classic Spanish spade but without any decoration and without flexibility at the juncture of mouthpiece and sidepiece. The other mass-produced bit with flat shanks is a grazing bit with ordinary port and elbow shanks. Its distinctive feature, making it an excellent bit for many purposes, is its extra hole for attachment of a curb strap behind the headstall hole at the top of the shank. The bend and the breadth of the shanks discourage lipping and their length gives proper, moderate leverage.

The shift away from the broad, flat cheekpieces, especially on spades and half-breeds, often taxes the ingenuity of modern horsemen to improvise lip-strap attachment, necessitated by the new shape of the shanks, which invites lipping but does not include lip-strap loops.

A

B

D

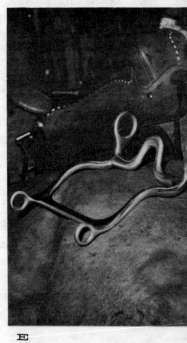

E

C

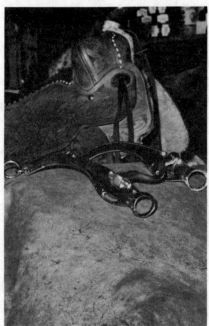

F

a. S-shanked spade; b. curb with copper cricket; c. curb with hooded cricket, currently very popular in the West; d. loose-shanked curb, port covered with copper wire; e. cast aluminum roping bit, currently popular; f. loose-shanked western curb. Courtesy of Troy's Western Store, Scottsdale, Arizona

I have one loose-jawed spade designed by a very highly esteemed bitmaker. It is made just right inside—smooth, comfortable spoon; good, smooth, copper coil braces curved well away from the horse's molars; and good, smooth, very flexible junctures of mouthpiece and sidepieces. The shanks incline slightly rearward as they drop from the mouthpiece, which is good. However, they are not flat but oval-shaped and not very broad. In fact, they are so narrow that they invite the investigative lips of a young horse so temptingly that I finally took a shoestring, tied one end to the rein ring on one side, passed it through the lip-strap ring of the curb chain and thence to the rein ring on the other side. This works fairly well, but I shall be very happy when I get my old Santa Barbara bit back from Garcias' where I sent it to have the worn braces replaced.

Exact replicas of the old Spanish bits of frontier days are still being made with fidelity to the last tiny star and minute concho by at least two establishments. Since they seem to stay in business, there must still be some demand for their products. The Garcia family of California has been making authentic bits for generations and make a wide assortment of curbs, half-breeds, and both rigid and loose-jawed spades. I recently saw a traveling display of the authentic Spanish and modern bits made by The Saddlery of Bakersfield. It included over sixty authentic designs. The Saddlery seems to be thriving; the Garcias still enjoy excellent patronage; and an authentic silver-mounted bit costs upwards of fifty dollars, so I suspect that not all the old-timers are riding the starry ranges and that some of their progeny still learn to use the old-style bits, in spite of the demands made on their time by compulsory public education.

The only fault I find with modern replicas of old-style bits is that the joints are what Xenophon called stiff. The mouthpieces are joined to the sidepieces by the authentic joints, but the fit is tighter.

21. AMERICAN INDIAN BITS

The American Indian's adoption of the horse and development of techniques for using him telescope into a few decades a re-enactment of several centuries of the earliest experience of mankind with horses. When the first mounted Spaniards encountered Indians, the aborigines were awestruck. They thought the mounted men were some kind of four-legged gods. For some time the very sight of a horseman struck terror into the natives. When, finally and inevitably, the Indians first saw a horse apart from a man, they still considered it a god, worshipped it and did some rather absurd things to propitiate and sustain it. When bands of horses began to run wild and forage for themselves on this continent, Indians first regarded them as food. Such was earliest man's first use of the horse. We have no proof that the first bit used by ancient man was a thong tied around the lower jaw, for thongs did not withstand the ravages of time to be discovered after ages by disturbers of the dead. However, the chances are pretty good that the first man of the steppes to straddle a horse probably, like the first American Indian to mount, used a thong around the jaw. Some of the oldest parts of a bit ever dug up were stone sidepieces found in Switzerland. These stone shanks were so shaped that the finders were fairly confident that they had been fashioned to be joined by a thong mouthpiece. I once saw in the Indian country that spreads across northeastern Arizona into New Mexico a squaw riding a horse, a rare thing indeed, for usually in those days it was only the male Indian who rose so high. This unique squaw was using as a bit a thong tied between two sticks. She may have been the only Indian who ever did such a thing, but she certainly illustrated a technique of her predecessors antedating her by several millennia.

Man's most distinctive characteristic according to Mark Twain is his cussedness. A more philanthropic commentator has said that man is unique because he is a symbol user and a lover of symbolic ritual. Such an evaluation is supported by the Indian's early use of the jaw thong on his horse. The way in which that thong was tied and the way in which it was decorated by a feather signified in what human activity the horse was used as a tool— war, hunting, or (one would suppose) courtship.

It was not long after the Indian began to ride that man's inhumanity to man left enough slaughtered cavalry mounts fully caparisoned on fields of battle to supply some Indians with steel bits of United States Cavalry issue. Many Indians were quick to take advantage of the good fortune, but others were good conservatives and stuck to the old jaw thongs. Today Scottsdale, Arizona, is treated at least once every year to the sight of Chief Bearstep, a highly respected resident of Scottsdale, riding in the Scottsdale rodeo parade mounted on his very magnificent Appaloosa stallion that wears a turquoise-studded bridle bearing a USC stamp on its bit. The Chief's saddle is barely recognizable as government issue of the last century, so studded is it with turquoise and silver. The Chief, now quite long in the tooth, tells how he inherited the saddle.

As far as I have been able to find out, the Indian has not ever invented a bit. His only innovation was in his technique of preparing the horse for use with a bit, and that is perhaps a repetition of ancient history rather than an innovation. The technique varied with geography and tribe, but the underlying principles were similar throughout the West. I offer here an account of my own observation of one instance of it.

One day I saw a scrawny little ewe-necked, dirty-brown equine tied with a short rope to a mesquite "tree." One eye was swollen shut. He could still see some out of the other, though it, too, had been bruised. Most of the hide of his head was intact, and he had not lost much hair or hide on the rest of his body. However, his sunken flanks indicated considerable dehydration. Learning that the animal was about ready for riding and would probably be mounted the next day, I returned to see the operation.

From the little group assembled to see the "fun," one male emerged. He was about the age at which our own youths, fortunately for horses, take to hot-rodding. He had a durable stick in each hand. When he was mounted, another member of the super-race attempted to untie the rope around the horse's head. In spite of considerable stimulation, the head hung so heavily on the rope and the knot was so tight that a knife was used to loosen the rope. Repeated whackings finally succeeded, and the animal staggered forward. The sticks, of course, were used for impulsion and for guiding. I did not wait to see how far the animal was made to travel. Nor did I ever learn the secret of how such a dehydrated horse could be given water without foundering.

I learned from a very old Indian that "in the day of many horses" an animal would be secured to a tree just as he was snared. If it happened to be by a foreleg, I assumed, the chances were pretty good that the leg would be broken. Nothing was lost, I learned—"Eat 'um" was the solution. Undoubtedly some of the more fortunate animals broke their necks or managed to choke themselves to death in spite of beatings and proddings from the rear to induce them to slacken the rope.

J. Frank Dobie, whose eye saw more and whose pen wrote more clearly than any others I have known, tells of more than one Indian pressed hard to put distance behind him. Such an Indian would take a mare and sucking colt if such were handy. The colt would serve for food. The mare would be driven to the point of diminishing return as a means of transportation. Then her blood would nourish the Indian. All this was accomplished without the use of a bit.

The preparation of a horse for use with a bit mentioned above —reducing him to a state of exhaustion and then guiding him by blows on the side of the head—and riding of the mare as far as she could go, related subsequently, probably parallel or re-enact man's earliest horsemanship thousands of years ago.

The Indian's horsemanship, like his political skill, has progressed farther in less than a century than the horsemanship of the bulk of mankind did in four thousand years. Today it is possible to see Indian horsemanship that rivals that of the best of the palefaces.

22. MODERN EVOLUTION OF THE BIT

A tenable assumption (which is gobbledygook for "a good guess") is that man first discovered he could use a horse for something other than food and clothing when some adolescent aborigine climbed onto the back of a maimed or exhausted horse, or tied a load of firewood to it, and found out that he could direct it by blows with a stick. (At least there is some indication that our American Indians took this route.) Soon, being a teenager, he wanted more action and tried a horse not quite so starved or crippled. He tied a thong in its mouth or tied a thong between sticks for a bit.

The probability is that this all happened somewhere in the great grassland that spreads, with some interruption by mountain ranges, from the Volga to the Danube. If they had food in their bellies, the tough little horses that roamed that country would probably put up a pretty good fight against any biped that tried to restrict or restrain them. So man invented a bit with claws on the sides and the roughest thing he could devise to hold the sidepieces together. The purpose of those early bits was undoubtedly to cause as much pain as possible. I can find little evidence there was much change in this cardinal principle of bit use for over a thousand years. The classical Greeks, with their slaves and high thinking, have left the earliest indications of a change in principle in bit use. Xenophon devised a bit that was probably capable of dealing more agony to a horse than had ever been previously achieved. According to his written word, the horse was first shown what the bit could do and then the bit, or a slightly less severe one, was used only as a threat. An easy inference from his writing is that he was the first or one of the first of horsemen to use the bit to communicate with the horse.

However, any communication between horse and horseman in those centuries preceding and immediately following the fruitful vision of the three wise men on the hills overlooking Bethlehem was a very rough sort of talk. Foam coming from the mouth of a horse wearing a bit was always bloody. An early Christian artist, so the story goes, was vexed at himself because he could not satisfactorily portray the bloody spume on the chest and neck of a horse in a picture he was painting. In a fit of vexation he grabbed up a sponge and threw it at the fresco. Behold! Just the effect he had been striving for—the sponge had been used to wipe up red pigment, and it hit the picture just behind the horse's bit.

We cannot trust painters too far for our conclusions about horsemanship, for one of them painted a picture of Xenophon some centuries after the great general had died. He pictured the horse as wearing a long-shanked curb bit, a kind of bit unknown in Greece until some time after Caesar brought one home from Flanders. However, there was truth in the painter's dirty sponge, for bits commonly produced red spume almost until the time of Pluvinel. The bit was the means of controlling the horse by fear, if not by constant pain, at least until after the time of Charles II's good friend, the Duke of Newcastle, who said, "Fear is the sure hold."

I can find no earlier evidence of change in this use of the bit as a means to control the horse by fear than a book written by Theodore A. Dodge, a Bostonian and a retired Civil War officer. Though an amputee, he served as his own model for illustrations of jumping and other feats of riding, and explained the superiority of his kind of horsemanship—establishing rapport and communication with a horse. In his book *Patrocles and Penelope* he indicates use of the bit for a wider range of performance, a greater versatility of the horse than any other writer about horsemanship seems to be aware of. Furthermore, for Dodge the horse's greatest role is that of being a means of sheer enjoyment, not a means of conspicuous consumption, or of competing in response to a challenge. So Dodge is probably the first really modern bit user.

Today there are many uses to which a horse is put, perhaps more than ever before in spite of the fact that he no longer is used in our part of the world as a means of transportation or power on farms or ranches. For some of these uses, the bit is employed in ways that smack of bygone days.

In an article in the September 1965 issue of *Horseman,* Jane Mayo, three times World's Champion Barrel Racer, advocates a gag bit, which she calls a draw bit. It resembles a snaffle inside the mouth, but the cannons are attached to either end of a centerpiece apparently about an inch long. This of course increases the pincher action. Round leather straps coming from the top of the horse's head slide freely through the sidepieces. This bit, says Jane Mayo, tends to make the corners of the colt's mouth sore, which she calls "an important part of starting a young horse."

The rodeo contestant sometimes uses a pain-causing bit to stop his rope horse. The polo player does so more frequently to stop his Thoroughbred. I have seen a winner of the five-gaited $10,000 stake at Louisville with red foam on its jaw.

The driver of the harness race horse uses the bit in a unique way that is little more than a century old. Ordinarily he uses neither pain nor fear but carries his horse in its learned gait by constant pressure on the bit, subtly varied.

Horsemen who strive for artificially high action, such as is seen in parade horses and Hackneys, usually impel their horses against a curb.

23. MODERN METHOD

To this list of distinctive but not entirely new uses of the bit today, I might add many more; but it is more important to turn to what is uniquely modern in the use of bits. The place to begin is with the preparation of the colt for this modern use, which depends neither on pain nor the threat of pain but on perfection of communication for its effectiveness. I personally feel that the bit can be used to its utmost as a means of communication only on a horse that has been handled from the day it was foaled by an intelligent horseman who understands thoroughly the method of bit use I am now considering. However, Henry Wynmalen, M.F.H., the author of some of the most valuable books in any horseman's library (and there is no modern horseman on record worthy of greater respect), seems quite willing to begin preparation for the bit after a young horse has been taught to lead and handled in other ways by competent but ordinary stable help. It is pertinent to add that Wynmalen is quite particular about the kind of horse he chooses.

Whether the preparation for the bit begins at foaling day or later, whether it is by the route of the snaffle or the jaquima, this *modern method* preparation is actually teaching a "language," a means of communication—not inculcation of fear. The horse is not physically equipped to use a verbal language like a human (though words, tones, or groups of words as signals can readily be learned by him). However, he is better equipped than a human to communicate by movement—kinesthetically. The knowledge of this fact and the use of that knowledge are what is uniquely modern in horsemanship, though several earlier horsemen, notably Xenophon, seem to have had suspicions about it. While all bodily movements of the rider, including those that are so obvious that the academic mind can recognize and catalog them as *aids,* are a part of this communication, none is more important or effective than the use of the bit. When, with the help of an intelligent horseman, the great light dawns on the young horse and movement of the bit becomes communication, not just something uncomfortable and threatening, he is "prepared for the bit"; he has, in Wynmalen's words, "accepted the bit." Obvious symptoms of this stage are the flexing at the poll and the light mouthing of the bit that is very different from the annoyed champing at the uncomfortable or threatening one.

The horseman learns with each horse the kinds of movements that will carry the message. Though there are certain common generalities that can be made, such as "raising the hand tends to lighten the forehand" (which communicates the direction, "get your hocks under you!"), each horse is unique. The horseman is supposed to be more intelligent than the horse and therefore should go more than halfway in finding the perfect kinesthetic communication for the particular horse he is handling.

When the communication has been established, it is maintained by movement and by the "passive resistance" to be discussed shortly, *never by a pulling at the reins.* Examples of the uselessness of pulling on the reins of the runaway (a horse that has been startled into a hysteria of running) are endless. Some months ago a very hotly bred young horse I was riding was thrown into a panic. The situation was such that I could not turn him (circling will sometimes stop the panic). I found, however, that he would respond to a lift of the forehand. The first movement of my hand got very slight response. I had sense enough not to increase the movement and try by force to get response. As I lifted him repeatedly in rhythm to his mad gallop, he began to respond and was soon coming up high enough in front to check his speed. Also, I got his attention. That squashed the hysteria.

I relate this incident not as a panacea for bolting horses (many of them have been mishandled so repeatedly that there is no cure that is not more costly than the price of a replacement for the horse) but to illustrate that the modern method does not include using the reins as a means of force—the forceful pull on the runaway is met by a forceful pull and more speed if any is left in the animal. I also hope to drive home the idea that kinesthetic communication, like verbal communication, is not made more understandable by increasing its volume. If a "word" is not understood, repeat it more distinctly (perhaps you were mumbling!). Sometimes it has to be repeated in rapid succession several times, as was my "word" to the hysterical youngster that was running so fast.

Teaching this kinesthetic language, preparing the horse for the bit or acceptance of the bit may be viewed by persons who have been exposed to the jargon of psychology as "conditioning the reflexes." I would rather say that it also involves a good deal of what modern educators try to do under the heading *reading readiness*. And there are no rigid rules to guide the educator. Some go the route of the snaffle, others the jaquima.

Wynmalen prepares a young and green horse to accept the snaffle, which is a prelude to the full bridle (double bridle, bit and bridoon, or curb and snaffle). Other equally modern users of the bit for purposes of communication only prepare a colt first for the jaquima as a long prelude to a curb or, in rare instances, to the spade.

There are many competent horsemen of both persuasions—
those who go the route of the snaffle and those who go the route
of the hackamore—who are less purely modern and turn out
excellent horses. However, being less modern, they pull the colt
about with the snaffle and frequently make the corners of his
mouth quite tender. Or they use the hackamore so severely that
they take a little hide, along with the hair, off his jaw. While
their horses may attain a degree of excellence, I believe that
horses trained by a purely modern method, which I shall attempt
to explain presently, are more versatile and enjoyable to use
though they may take a little longer to "make." This modern
method, however, does not prepare the horse for use by the
careless and the ignorant, as an experience of mine taught me.

A WESTERN COMPROMISE

When I first saw a little bunch of feral horses, which had been
caught on the desert near Red Rock, Arizona (an area long since
denuded of wild bands), "rough broke" for sale, I, being young
and brash, insisted to a friend who had brought me to witness
"the fun" that there was no need to handle any horse so brutally.
I said that any wild horse could be made into an obedient mount
by other and more modern means.

"Why," I averred, "John Rarey did it three-quarters of a
century ago."

"Yes," replied my older and wiser friend, "but the easy-broke
horse will buck when you get him in a tight place. The buck is
in 'em, and it better come out at the start. I wouldn't give a damn
for a horse that didn't have some buck in him."

Some days later my friend rode by and said, partly as a gesture
of friendship and partly to call my hand, "There's a three-year-
old down in Joe Avenente's trap that's coming to me. I don't
want to bother with him now. You can have him if you'll go
down and get him."

I expressed my gratitude, and my friend rode on.

As soon as I could saddle a good, steady horse I was on my
way to the Avenente trap.

With the impatience of the young, I was a bit too hasty in getting a halter on the young animal. I approached him instead of letting him make all the advances. My good gelding got the broomtail to my corral without much difficulty. Then I used a compromised and shortened version of the new method to prepare the horse for the bit.

In a few days I turned the young mustang over to a horseman of not much experience but more than ordinary intelligence. He was getting along fine with the youngster, but business called him away for a few days. When he returned, he thought perhaps before he rode the colt again he had better let a more experienced horseman ride him first. A cowboy friend obliged. That mustang promptly bucked off not only the cowboy but also the saddle and bridle!

This was the second of my two attempts to use an abridgment of the new method to prepare a wild horse for the bit. Later I used the new method without compromise or hurry on two other feral horses trapped off the range. Both of them have given years of service without bucking, and one has played a little amateur polo, though I did not prepare him for use of the kind of bit the polo player used on him.

These experiences illustrate that the new method cannot be compromised or abridged and that it does not prepare the horse for rough and careless handling.

A colt's first experience with man, I feel, is extremely important. It determines for him what kind of a thing man is and molds the young animal's attitude toward that thing. This first conception of man can be altered by subsequent treatment, but rarely and only by slow and patient work on the part of a good horseman can it be altered so that the animal becomes more pleasantly amenable to human wishes. The colt's conception of man can of course quickly be shattered by an ignorant handler and the colt turned into an "onery critter" to be conquered only by the roughest of old-fashioned uses of the bit—and some other things.

I like to start preparation of the colt for a bit just as soon as he is able to stand on all four legs and get them in motion more

or less harmoniously. At this time, one use of the hand so justifiably emphasized and well-explained by Wynmalen is vitally
important. In such use, the hand does not pull. It is a thing of
passive resistance, like a post. However, it is a post that moves
with the colt.

PREPARING THE LITTLE COLT

In my right hand (acting as one post), over the baby's loins,
I hold the ends of a loop of rope that goes behind his stifles. In
my left hand (also a post that moves with him) I hold a light
shank close to his halter. The first move is his. Later he can learn
to start when the post starts and stop when it stops. The move
may be immediate or it may take several minutes. The posts do
not move until he does. Then they move just fast enough to
allow him to walk briskly or trot slowly. At this first move, they
may even allow for a pretty brisk rate of speed for a spurt, for
I don't want to start a fight if I can avoid it. If there is one, the
hands (posts) do not pull or yank, they merely resist passively.

Many months later—years, in fact—these first roles of the
loop of rope and halter will be played by the legs of a rider and
a bit, the former to define impulsion (the good horseman always
carries his horse ahead of the rider's legs) and the latter to
define restraint and balance.

There may be, probably will be, a few little cavorts and kicks
necessitating some readjustment of the loop, but soon the baby,
far superior in intelligence to his human brother of like age, will
get the hang of the arrangement and will take quite a few steps
in a more or less orderly fashion. That's enough. I do not want
to tax his little patience the first day.

As soon as the baby and I have established an agreement about
this walking with me at his shoulder, I tie the loose end of the
halter shank to the side of his halter opposite me. So I have a
pair of reins instead of a shank. I leave a long end of shank
hanging from the new knot, and it serves as a sort of emergency
shank held in my left post in addition to the rein. I hold rein

and emergency shank about midway between poll and withers several inches above the tiny neck.

Now the left post (hand) occasionally moves to one side— right side for right turn, left side for left turn—and the baby soon responds to neckreining. Wynmalen in his *Dressage* (the most valuable book in any horseman's library, whether he is interested in dressage or not—the title is deceptive) seems to me to play down the importance of neckreining, not mentioning it until explaining mounted work. I start it as early as possible. Response to the lateral pull, the plow rein, is learned easily and usually instantly on a lunge line or from the sadde.

I prefer working a colt while I am mounted on a responsive, steady horse to work on a lunge line. I handle the colt first on one side, then on the other, using my hand above him much as I would use it if I were riding him. However, most horsemen find it easier and more convenient to use a lunge line. Again, with the lunge line, the postlike function of the hand is important, though with a playful colt it sometimes has to give way instantly to prevent a cavort from becoming a turn on the forehand that might bow a young tendon.

Wynmalen and other good horsemen do much work on the longlines in preparation for use of the bit. Both it and the lunge line can be used to cultivate response to lateral use of the bit and to start to increase the vocabulary of the language of the bit. Slight movements of the post as signals, always consistently employed, are quickly interpreted.

INTRODUCTION OF BIT

There is lack of agreement among good horsemen about the proper time for first putting a bit into a young horse's mouth. Certainly none of them would put a bit in the colt's mouth before he has learned to respond to a lead shank in the hand of a man walking at his shoulder. Few would put the bit in the mouth before the colt has learned to work well on the lunge line, starting, stopping, reversing, and changing speed on signal. Most horsemen, among those who use the longlines, would start with the bit when first using the lines.

Whatever the time of first putting the bit into the mouth, the latter should be treated carefully. Wynmalen uses the adverb "tenderly." Unless a young horse is first thoroughly educated with a jaquima, and sometimes even if he has been, the first bit in his mouth is a snaffle or a soft, leather-covered bar. Wynmalen cautions against "nervous injury" to the mouth, advocating a running martingale for use with a snaffle when the colt is first mounted. If one is used, the snaffle must be provided with two pairs of reins, one free and the other through a martingale adjusted so that it comes into play only if the colt's head is tossed up higher than his normal head carriage.

No good horseman tries to teach a colt until it is in good physical condition. He, like all good educators, knows that learning can only flourish when the learner is feeling fit. So the colt that is "full of himself" is the one that learns best. Also, he is the one that is most apt to injure his mouth accidentally. Because this is so, I am very glad to have learned from Southwestern horsemen the use of the jaquima. While others get excellent results from using the cavesson on the lunge line in preparing for the bit, which they must use as soon as the horse is mounted or driven, I find it much easier to get the results I want with the new method of prolonging the pre-bit education by use of the jaquima. I even prefer it to the cavesson when using the lunge line or working the yearling from the back of another horse.

Earlier in this book I have briefly described the usual method of hackamore training, and in *Out of the West* I have given a more detailed explanation. With the new method the hackamore is used without its employment for coercion. No hair or hide need be disturbed on the jaw, if it is in good hands and time enough is taken to let the horse understand what is wanted before he is asked to perform with speed and precision. With its use, the horse becomes accustomed to the bit long before he is asked to learns its "language." He only knows its language when he will, as Wynmalen so aptly puts it, "flex with a smile and champ the bit" on a slack rein while the rider holds the reins lightly in sensitive fingers, with arm or arms hanging comfortably down from the shoulders, neither clamped in against his sides nor arms akimbo, wrists bent inward just enough to destroy rigidity of a straight line from elbow to finger knuckles (thumb knuckles up). Those sensitive fingers, through the variations of the slack of the reins, understand what the horse is communicating by the movement of his bars, just as the horse is interpreting the mind of his rider by the movements of the fingers affecting the slack so imperceptibly that no onlooker is aware the fingers are active.

For some purposes where the range of activity required of a horse is limited and therefore the range of communication is small, as for instance in a hunting field where the activity ranges from keeping up with the pack to keeping behind the huntsman, a snaffle bit is adequate for such communication. It is probably better suited to some hands than any other bits, especially if it is equipped with two pairs of reins, one through a running martingale properly adjusted (never used with the curb of a double bridle by any but the ignorant and the ineffectual and never used with the snaffle of the double bridle by any but the inexperienced). However, for the rider who enjoys the full range of equine performance and for the horse that knows the whole range of the "language of the bit," the full bridle is the only equipment. The vocabulary of that language is limited when the curb is used alone—more so when the snaffle only is used. On the military trumpet, devoid of valves and limited to the notes of the triad, quite a tune can be played, but with the cornet or the orchestral trumpet provided with valves and capable of all the tones and half tones of the scale, many more tunes can be played.

Some unexcelled horsemen I know will deny the superiority of the English full bridle and communicate with their finished mounts through a loose-jawed spade, the most delicate of all bits. To them I bow and stand corrected, for in their hands that bit has a complete vocabulary—all the tones and half tones of the scale—and it has a big advantage for the horse because his mouth can more easily move its shanks than those of the English curb, which gives him no leverage and nothing but a small round bar with a slight crook in it to manipulate.

As is evident in many places in this book, the snaffle is most useful in communicating about movements of the horse that are extended, with balance forward, while the curb is most useful about those in which collection is involved. In using the two in conjunction, the entire range of equestrian activity is covered.

I am not forgetting the word of any good user of the spade who might do me the honor of comment. It would be to this effect: Your case for the full bridle is from the point of view of the rider's communication *to* the horse and does not take into account the superiority of the spade in communication a good hand gets *from* the horse. My answer to that voice is, for you the spade is tops, but for any but the one pair of hands among ten thousand a spade is disastrous to both horse and rider. Almost any ambitious rider can learn to use the double bit with at least a modicum of success and more safety than he enjoys in a car.

24. BITS FOR THE AVERAGE RIDER

The horse, the most timid and at the same time the most readily excitable of all domestic animals, is a marvelous creature. Thousands of people who use him for transportation into places of scenic beauty inaccessible by any other means sit on him like a sack of potatoes, kick his sides like a football to start him forward, tug at the reins like a sailor on a line to stop him, and move their hands lackadaisically to the side to turn him. And he gets them into the primitive areas and gets them back to tea or cocktails in perfect safety—and with few blisters and bruises. In the West, horses that earn thier keep by so doing are usually equipped with a grazing bit, a curb of moderate length of curved shank. Ordinarily it is provided with a strap, not a chain. This strap is usually longer than I have prescribed as the proper length to avoid pinching the corners of the mouth. Rarely has the owner thought or cared to put the top of the bit shank in a vise and bend it outward so the strap will not pinch. Usually the horse takes the pinch on the calloused corners of his mouth without comment. On rare occasions when his rider hangs onto the reins for some length of time, he may toss his head in the air in mild protest. Much of the time he is following the horse ahead of him, so his rider is content to let the reins hang.

The range of equestrian skill, between those riders of the dude strings and horsemen using the full bridle for communication as nearly perfect as possible, is wide. Midway between them are the host of American riders (and probably many in other lands I am not fortunate enough to know personally) who have neither the time nor the inclination to cultivate their equestrian skill to its utmost. Nevertheless, these riders enjoy riding and are fond of their mounts. Their concern with bits, those of them who ride amenable horses that have had intelligent training, is to find the bit most suitable to their hands. Each of them has a unique problem in doing so, which he must solve if he is to get the maximum satisfaction from his use of his horse. For most such riders, or at least those who are willing to use double reins, the four ring Pelham with a seven-inch shank, properly adjusted (and provided with a lip strap if it is an English bit) is most satisfactory. I have seen some riders who did not like to use double reins, who rode with a bit converter on a four-ring Pelham and found it very satisfactory. The bit converter, listed in better catalogs, is a short, round strap with buckled loops at either end. One end buckles into the top ring of the Pelham and the other into the bottom ring. The rein then is attached to the evener, on which it slides freely. I frowned on this device until I saw it used so satisfactorily by friends who ride well-trained, mature horses and hate the bother of double reins.

Most Western riders who ride with moderate skill find the single rein and the mild Western curb very satisfactory. Its backward bend of shank goes well with the high hand necessitated by the horn of a Western saddle. The variety of mouthpieces and of shanks available is large, and the rider who experiments until he finds the exact bit best suited to his hand will get the most enjoyment possible from his riding.

BITS FOR RIDERS WITH PROBLEMS

Some horsemen for the sake of economy or other reasons ride horses that have been unfortunate in their early training and therefore have habits or vices that are problems. For such problems, the skilled trainer might use a full bridle, if the horse is worth the time and trouble to correct the fault. For the average rider, proper choice of a special bit will often solve the problem or at least lessen it sufficiently to enable the rider to get enjoyable service from his mount.

On the horse that pulls and is hard to hold, the solution is a milder bit than he is used to and dexterous use of hands. However, lacking dexterity, the rider may solve the problem by use of the special cavesson described earlier in this book—one consisting of two curb chains that cross under the jaw and are attached to the studded nosepiece of leather. Another solution may be one of the numerous hackamore bits now offered for sale. Most of these have nothing that goes inside the mouth of the horse but if properly adjusted can have a powerful leverage on his nose and jaw. Such a device must be so adjusted that it presses on the nose just *above* the soft cartilage and also so that the shank will, when the reins are pulled tight, come back to a 45-degree angle with the mouth, and *no more than a 45-degree angle*. As a rule, severe bits on the pulling horse merely add fuel to flame or make the horse exchange one vice for a worse one.

The horse that gets behind the bit, that is, overcollects with a tendency to come up in front or back up at the slightest touch on the reins when he is excited, will usually be corrected or at least made more pleasant to handle if a hackamore bit is used on him. Sometimes a leather-covered or rubber bit used with one pair of reins free and the other through a running martingale will work wonders on such a horse.

The head tosser is usually a horse that has been ridden with a curb strap or chain so loose that it pinched the corners of his mouth. In other instances, he is a horse that has been ridden with a severe bit of some sort, or by a heavy-handed rider. The cure is first to remove the cause. Then either a standing martingale can be used or a running martingale with one pair of reins (which must be either those of a snaffle or the top reins of a four-rein Pelham—*never* the curb reins or the bottom reins of the four-rein Pelham—run through it.

The horse that rears should never be ridden by the inexperienced rider without suicidal intentions. However, a standing martingale properly adjusted provides about the only element of safety possible in riding him.

A gag bit is about the only aid for the borer and the runaway, though only the foolhardy and the extremely experienced (he only if the horse is so valuable he is worth much trouble) will venture on his back.

The list of bits for special purposes might be explained indefinitely. To find the best bit for each particular case requires diligent search and experiment, though the accomplished horseman rarely finds need for more than a double bridle. The perfect bit for every hand on every horse has not yet been invented, and the probability that it ever will be is as remote as the probability that man will learn to live with his fellows in peace and mutual understanding.

The horseman, experienced or not, who respectfully and earnestly strives always to understand what his horse is communicating to him on the bit (and by other means), will improve his equestrian skill with every hour he spends on a horse, and he may find that a change in bits is a temporary advantage.

 **GLOSSARY**

AMERICAN SADDLE HORSE—A breed of horse originating in America, now best known as a three- or five-gaited show horse.

BAR (S)—(1) Lower jaw of a horse between bridle teeth and molars.
(2) Irons of a saddle to which stirrup leathers are attached.

BAR BIT—Driving bit with straight or slightly curved solid mouthpiece.

BEARING REINS—Strap to make a horse in harness hold his head high. It is attached at either side of a bit, then run through metal loops on bridle located just below the ears, then through a hook at the top of the backband of the harness.

BEHIND THE BIT—Overresponsive to the bit.

BITTING RIG—Harness used by some trainers in schooling young horses. Usually consists of a surcingle, back strap, crupper, overcheck, sidereins, and bridle.

BORER—A horse that continually pulls on the bit by thrusting his head forward and downward.

BOSAL—Specially designed noseband, usually of braided rawhide or horsehair. Also called "bozal."

BREAST COLLAR—Part of driving harness, a wide strap around the front of the shoulders just below juncture of the neck, held up by narrower strap over the withers.

BRIDOON—A snaffle bit.

BUCK LINE—Line used in multiple draft hitches to keep a horse from getting ahead of his mate. It was attached to the draw chain.

BURR—A round piece of leather or plastic two or three inches in diameter faced with bristles. It fits around a bit just inside the cheekpiece and irritates the corner of a horse's mouth.

BUXTON BIT—A curb bit used in a carriage harness (heavy harness bit).

CANNON—The part of a bit from the joint of the mouthpiece to the sidepiece, or cheekpiece. The part of a horse's leg from the pastern joint to the knee.

CAVESSON—Noseband.

CHEEKPIECE—The part of a bit that is outside a horse's mouth; also the part of a bridle that runs from bit to crownpiece.

CHECK REIN—Strap used on either side of a bitting rig to make a horse hold his chin in.

CHECKREIN—Strap used in driving to make a horse hold his head high; goes from bit up the front of the face, between the ears, and fastens to the hook on top of the backstrap.

COLLECTION—Getting a horse to flex his neck and get his weight or balance farther to the rear than usual.

COLT BIT—A very loose term now used to designate any bit thought to be useful on a colt, such as the jointed Pelham. In horse-and-buggy days the *Moseman Catalog* listed colt bits only as rings of steel that completely encircled the lower jaw, sometimes provided with "keys" the colt could mouth.

CRICKET—A small roller in the port of a curb bit (common only in Western bits).

CROWNPIECE—Part of a bridle that goes over a horse's head behind his ears.

CURB—Any bit making use of the principle of the lever and fulcrum, a Weymouth bit.

DEMIPASSADE—A passade was a movement of the classical riding halls of the sixteenth century, the *manège,* in which the horse traversed back and forth over a specified short straight track making alternate changes of direction at either end, done in various speeds and gaits. A demipassade was a movement, very fast, down the track, a quick reversal, and a return.

DEXTER—Any of several patented driving bits; one variety was a snaffle with a ring attached to encircle the lower jaw. It was, of course, without leverage and not to be confused with the Moorish ring bit.

DOCKED—Having the tail bone amputated a few inches from the body.

DOUBLE BRIDLE—Bridle equipped with both curb and snaffle bits. Also called FULL BRIDLE or BIT and BRIDOON BRIDLE.

DRAWREIN—Strap or rope attached to girth or other part of saddle or harness, run through the bit ring and thence to the hand of the rider or driver.

DRENCHING BOTTLE—A long-necked bottle used to make a horse swallow liquid medicine. Never used by veterinarians and frequently the cause of death by foreign body pneumonia when used by others.

DUMB JOCKEY—A type of bitting rig.

ECHINI—Spiked rollers on the mouthpiece of a Grecian bit. Also called HEDGEHOG.

EGG BUTT—Termination of either end of a mouthpiece of a bit in a barrel-shaped joint.

FAST REIN—Quick response to rein.

FIADOR—Also called THEODORE, a modern corruption. A small rope around the throttle passing through the ends of the browband and knotted to the end of a bosal to keep it from dropping below the chin.

FLAT SADDLE—English-type saddle, one without high pommel or cantle.

FULL BRIDLE—A bridle equipped with a curb and snaffle, a fall bridle.

GAG BIT—Any bit used with a gag rein. Some have rings especially designed to facilitate freedom of the gag rein. This bit puts pressure on the corners of the mouth, not on the bars.

GAG REIN—Rein fastened at the top of the bridle and running freely through the bit rings.

GALLOWAYS—One of the types of small, easy-riding horses highly prized in England prior to the seventeenth century.

GAUCHOS—Natives of the South American pampas.

GIG—A two-wheeled vehicle once used for country driving.

GRAND CIRCUIT—A program of harness racing on the major tracks that flourished in American cities early in this century.

GREAT HORSE—The big horse Caesar found the natives using in England, the ancestor of Shires and Clydesdales.

HACKAMORE—A loose term used to designate almost anything put on a horse's head except a bridle with conventional bit or a manufactured halter.

HACKAMORE BIT—A noseband attached to a lever and chain. The noseband's pressure makes the nose act like a fulcrum, the chin like a weight. Thus, the device uses the lever principle as a curb bit does, but without a mouthpiece.

HACKNEY—A breed of horse originating in England. It is characterized by extremely high action.

HALF-BREED BIT—Any curb bit with a high port provided with a cricket, common in the Southwest.

HANOVERIAN—(1) A horse whose lineage traces to Hanover, considered by some as the founder of the American Thoroughbred.

(2) A curb bit jointed at either side of the port and provided with rollers on the cannons.

HEADSTALL—A bridle without bits attached.

HEDGEHOG—Another name for the ECHINI, the spiked roller mouthpiece of early Greek bits.

HEEL KNOT—The terminal knot of a bosal, to which reins and lead rope are usually attached.

HERMOSILLO BIT—A Mexican curb, always handmade, with very loose curved cheekpiece and a port provided with a cricket. This bit has a distinctive silver inlaid design on the shanks or cheekpieces.

HOBBIES—A breed of small, easy-gaited horse originating in Ireland, highly prized prior to the seventeenth century.

JAQUIMA—Hackamore.

JERK LINE—The single line by which the lead horse of freight team was controlled.

J.I.C. BIT—A patented driving bit, very severe. To each cheekpiece is jointed a mouthpiece of small diameter. The free end of each mouthpiece protrudes through the cheekpiece to which it is not attached and terminates in a small ring for attachment of driving line.

LATERAL GAIT—A gait in which two feet on each side make impact with the ground at the same or nearly the same time, as in the pace and the stepping pace.

LEVADE—A movement fashionable in the classic riding halls. It consists of squatting on the hind quarters and raising the forelegs off the ground.

LIPPING THE BIT—Using the lower lip to get the shank or sidepiece of a curb bit into the mouth.

LUNGE LINE (or longe line)—A strap, rope or substitute about thirty feet long with snap or swivel on one end. Used for exercising or training by having the animal describe a circle around the handler.

MANÈGE—(1) A riding school or hall.

(2) Movements the horse performs in such a place.

MARTINGALE, RUNNING—Y-shaped strap having one end attached to girth or cinch and the other ends terminating in rings through which the reins run.

MARTINGALE, STANDING—Strap having one end attached to girth or cinch and the other attached to a noseband.

MONTE FOREMAN BIT—A Western bit designed by the popular horseman, Monte Foreman. Its most distinctive detail is the extra rings attached to the headstall rings. These extra rings are for the curb chain or strap and keep the chain or strap from pinching the corners of the mouth.

NECKREIN—To guide a horse by moving the bridle hand in the direction the rider desires to turn the horse.

OVERCHECK (checkrein)—A strap to make a horse hold his head up. It goes from the bit up the horse's face, between his ears, and attaches to a hook on top of the backband of a driving harness.

PALFREY—An easy-gaited, small horse used by English gentlefolk for transportation prior to the seventeenth century.

PHAETON—A very comfortable, four-wheeled buggy commonly used by people of means as transportation in cities before the advent of the automobile.

PILLARS—Heavy posts set just wide enough apart to permit a horse to stand, or prance, between them. After securely tying the horse between the pillars, the trainer whipped or otherwise excited the horse to make him perform.

PLOW REIN—Guiding a horse by lateral pull, rather than by neckrein.

POLL—Highest point of a horse's head.

PORT—An upward curve in the center of the mouthpiece of a curb bit.

PSALION—Called "the crooked cavesson" in the *Palatine Anthology*. A cavesson of classical Greece resembling our hackamore bits.

PULLEY BIT—A bit provided with pulleys for a gag rein. One ingenious one was designed for the use of the gag on one side only—still a puzzle to modern students on the history of horse gear.

QUARTER HORSE—A breed of horse for which a registry was established in America in 1940. It is presumed to be very fast for a quarter of a mile.

REGULATOR—Any one of several devices used on a harness race horse to prevent side pulling.

REMUDA—A band of horses used on a roundup.

RING BIT—The Moorish, Arabian, or Mexican ring bit has a ring running loosely through the upper end of its high port, and around the lower jaw. This ring acts like a fulcrum and the shanks like a lever when reins are pulled.

ROSADERA (Spanish, *rozadera*)—A rather loose term usually designating a detail of horse or mule gear that rubs against the hair. Specifically used to designate the parts of a jaquima that contacts the lower jaw of a horse, the shanks.

ROWEL—The revolving part of a spur.

SADDLE HORSE, SADDLER—Terms popularly used for a horse of the American Saddle Horse breed.

SIDE PULLER—A horse (most frequently a race horse) that continually pulls harder on one side of the bit than on the other.

SIDECLAWS—Sharp projections on the inside of the sidepieces of a bit to cause pain on the outside of the mouth.

SIDEPIECE—The part of a bit that is outside a horse's mouth.

SNAFFLE—A bit without leverage, having a jointed mouthpiece.

SPADE—A bit with leverage like a curb but having in place of a port a high spoon or spade containing a cricket and connected to the cheekpieces by copper braces.

SPOON—The projection arising from the center of a spade bit mouthpiece, from three to four inches long, and about an inch and a half wide near its upper extremity.

SUFFOLK PUNCH HORSE—Smallest of the British draft breeds.

SURCINGLE—Band encircling a horse just behind his forelegs.

TAIL SET—A rigid contraption of metal to keep a horse's tail in an unnatural position while he is in his stall so that he will hold it high when he is ridden or driven. Unfortunately, it is forbidden by law in only a few states.

THORN BIT—A very severe bit with spiked mouthpiece said to be still in use in some parts of the Orient.

THOROUGHBRED—A breed of horse originating in England and used principally for racing and hunting.

TRAP—A two-wheeled vehicle designed for country driving.

VAQUERO—Mexican cowboy.

VOLTE—A movement of the classical riding halls. The hooves of the horse executed two parallel circles or squares with round corners.

WALKER—An American breed of horse, the Tennessee Walking Horse.

WALKING HORSE BIT—A curb bit with shanks, usually S-shaped, seven to nine inches long.

WEYMOUTH—A curb bit with straight shanks provided with lip strap rings.

 # REFERENCES —
A PARTIAL LISTING

(*This list does not include standard histories, encyclopedias, and other such source material used in writing this book.*)

ANDERSON, K. *Ancient Greek Horsemanship.* Berkeley: University of California Press, 1961.

APSLEY, VIOLA LADY. *Bridleways through History.* London: Hutchinson & Co., 1926.

BARRETTO DE SOUZA, J. M. T. *Principles of Equitation.* New York: E. P. Dutton & Co., 1922.

BEACH, BELLE. *Riding and Driving for Women.* New York: Charles Scribner's Sons, 1912.

CERAM, C. W. *The Secret of the Hittites.* New York: Alfred A. Knopf, 1956.

COOLIDGE, DANE. *Old California Cowboys.* New York: E. P. Dutton & Co., 1939.

DEL VILLAR, JOSE ALVAREZ. *Historia de la Charreria.* Mexico City: Londres, 1941.

DOBIE, J. FRANK. *The Mustangs.* New York: Little, Brown & Co., 1952.

DODGE, THEODORE A. *Patrocles and Penelope.* New York: Houghton, Mifflin & Co., 1885.

FAIRSERVIS, WALTER A., JR. *The Origins of Oriental Civilization.* New York: New American Library, 1959.

FORBES, ESTHER. *Paul Revere.* Boston: Houghton Mifflin Co., 1942.

GILBEY, SIR WALTER. *The Great Horse.* London: Vinton & Co., 1899.

GRAHAM, R. B. CUNNINGHAME. *The Horses of the Conquest,* ed. ROBERT MOORMAN DENHARDT. Norman: University of Oklahoma Press, 1949.

HUS, ALAIN. *The Etruscans.* New York: Grove Press, 1951.

LEA, TOM. *The Hands of Cantu.* New York: Little, Brown & Co., 1964.

LHOTE, HENRI. *The Search for the Tassili Frescoes.* New York: E. P. Dutton & Co., 1959.

LITTAUER, VLADIMIR S. *Horseman's Progress.* New York: D. Van Nostrand Co., 1962.

MARVIN, CHARLES. *Training the Trotting Horse.* New York: The Marvin Publishing Co., 1891.

MORA, JO. *Trail Dust and Saddle Leather.* New York: Charles Scribner's Sons, 1950.

RAWLINSON, GEORGE. *The Five Great Monarchies of the Ancient Eastern World,* Vol. I. New York: Dodd, Mead, & Co., 1891.

RICE, TAMARA TALBOT. *The Scythians.* London: Thames & Hudson, 1957.

"SCRUTATOR." *Horses and Hounds.* London: George Routledge & Co., 1958.

SELF, MARGARET CABELL. *The Horseman's Encyclopedia.* New York: A. S. Barnes Co., Inc., 1946.

TAYLOR, LOUIS. *Out of the West.* New York: A. S. Barnes Co., Inc., 1965.

————. *Ride American.* New York: Harper & Row, 1963.

WARD, FAY E. *The Cowboy at Work.* New York: Hastings House, 1958.

WYNMALEN, HENRY. *Dressage.* New York: A. S. Barnes Co., Inc., 1952.

INDEX

Action, artificially high, 31, 32, 184
American Horse and Mule Breeders Association, 158
American Indian, 177–180
American Quarter Horse Registry, 83
American Show Horse under Flat Saddle, 143
Apsley, Lady, 87, 90
Arabians, 141
Arabs, cheekpiece designs, 83, 84, 167
Argentina and Egyptian noseband, 97, 167
Art of Horsemanship, The, 69–72
Ashleigh bit, 107, 108, 109
Assyria, 43, 47, 52, 53; and curb bits, 75

Babylonians, 26, 36
Baja California, 19, 20, 72, 164
Balance, and the bit, 29–30; and dumb jockey, 103; as key to riding and driving, 8–10
Bar bits, ancient, 39, 80; for draft horses, 157, 158–159; for driving, 114; and harness race horses, 104
Bars, horse's, and communication, 193
Basques, 80
Bass, Tom, 148
Bit, and American Indian, 177–180; burr, 129, 131; and communication, 7–8, 30, 166, 182, 193–194; converter, 196; guards, 152; holder, Sure Win,, 120–121; introducing colt to, 191–193; modern use of, 185–194; response to, 29–30; role of, 4–5, 28; suited to each horse, 7–8, 90; types of, for average riders, 195–197; bone, 73; Bronze Age, 58–59; Buxton, 107, 108, 109; Cavalry, 135–136; 169–171; Charlie Dunn, 146, 147–148; coaching, 103–104, 107, 108, 156; colt, 172; carriage, 107–111; corrective, 115, 150–151, 197–198; for cowboys, 163–169; Dexter snaffle ring bit, 118, 120; double, 144–145, 183, 194; double-twisted wire, 115; for draft horses, 156–160; draw, 183; for driving, 113–120; early, 18–26, 49, 79–82; egg butt,

114; of Egypt, 38, 39, 41, 43; English curb, 91–92; flexible, 104, 106, 107; full cheek, 95; gag, 131, 140, 183, 198; grazing, 195–196; for Great Horse, 85, 86; Greek hedgehog, 23, 66, 72, 106; half-breed, 167, 172–173; Hanoverian roller mouth Pelham, 69, 138; for harness racing, 122–124; Hermosillo, 168; J.I.C., 116, 118; leverage, 169; loose-hawed, 104, 105, 106; medicine, 160–161; Monte Foreman, 149; mouthing, English, 69; for mules, 115, 157, 166; overcheck, 114, 120–122, 124–128; Philips Safety, 122; pulley, 131; Regulator, 129, 131–132; for Renaissance horses, 87–88; ring, 79–80, 82, 166; roller mouth, 61, 69, 138; Roman, 73–78; for show ring, 144–145; Spanish, 79, 163, 176; Springsteen, 118; thong, 18, 73, 178; thorn, 97; Tom Bass, 147, 148–149; for Walking Horse, 115, 151–153; western, 172–173, 176; wooden, 162; Xenophon's, 70–72, 79, 104
Biting, 162
Bitting, harness, 102; rig, and rearing, 43
Blaze, 31
Bosal, 18, 38, 39, 64–65; *see also* Jaquima
Bridle, double, 145–149; early Greek, 59; Egyptian, 39; full, 88, 98, 134; assembling, 13–14; and cavesson, 95; and fox-hunting, 98; playing with bits, 106; Greek chariot racing, 62; Numidian oxen, 41
Bridle Ways Through History, 87
Bridoon, with bearing rein, 113; defined, 97; for hunter or jumper, 153, 155; Irish, 98–100
Bronze Age, bits of, 58–59
Brown, Major Harry, 99
Bucephalus, 52
Buck line, 44
Bucking and wild horses, 188–189
Burr, bit, 129, 131
Buxton bit, 107, 108, 109

Caesar, 76–79, 82, 84–85

130–132; ancient, 62, 77; in England, 94–95; and gag rein, 118; and reins, 95
Ranch and dude guest, 65–66
Rarey, John S., 116, 162, 188
Raymond Leverage Chin Check, 124–125, 128
Rearing, 29–30, 198
Regulator bits, 129, 131–132
Rein(s), bearing, 110–111; double, 196; Egyptian use of, 43–47; gag, 118; and language, 8; slack, and light hand, 64, 65, 66, 106; "sliding," 93; and Sumerians, 35; and trotters, 124; use of four, 87
Renaissance art, horses in, 87
Riders, average, 195–197
Riding schools, 87–91
Ring bit, 79–80, 82; and cowboys, 166; Dexter snaffle, 118, 120
Rock paintings, Sahara, 24, 38–39 fn.
Rocky Fork Hunt Club, 98–100
Rodeos, 172, 183
Roller mouth bits, 61, 69, 138
Rollers, copper, 167; spiked, 68–69; and Xenophon's bits, 70–72
Roman Empire, 73, 75–77, 78; and *psalion*, 21–22
Royal Studs, 96
Russell, Charles, 169
Russia, bits from, 38

Saddle gaits, 32–33, 76
Saddlery, The, 176
Santa Barbara spade bit, 84, 176
Sarmatians, 25
Sculpture, earliest horse, 49, 63
Scythians, 25, 26, 29, 49
Self, Margaret Cabell, 167
Semites, 26
Serfs, bits of, 85–86
Shire, 77, 85
Show ring, bits for, 144–145; and gimmicks, 31; holding reins, 49; *levade*, 30
Simon, 72, 78
Sloan, Tod, 130
Snaffle, and Celtish bit, 97; and colt, 102, 169, 187–188; for double bridle, 149; for draft horses, 157, 158–159; driving, 113; and Duke of Newcastle, 91; egg butt, 114, 130; and Egyptian bits, 49, 59, 95; and extension, 194; full cheek, 130; Greek bits, 58, 80; for hunting, 193; leather-covered, 192; for race horses, 95, 118, 120,

122, 131–132; for riding horses, 130; ring bit, Dexter, 118, 120; for running horses, 114; of serfs, 86; use of, 88
"Snatching back," 63
Spade bits, correct use, 165–166; invention of, 82–83; loose-jawed, 165–176, 193–194; misuse of, 84; modern, 83–84, 173; Santa Barbara, 84; and Southwest, 97; training with, 71–72, 164
Spaniards, 97, 163–164
Spanish Riding School of Vienna, 92
Speed, key to, 8, 124
Springsteen bit, 118
Stud Book, 97
Suffolks, 85, 160
Sumerians, 26, 28
Sure Win bit holder, 120–121
Switzerland, 25, 38

Tartars, 25
Temperament, horse's, and bits, 7–8
Tennessee Walking Horse, 143, 144, 151; bits of, 115, 151–153; brutal training of, 31, 92; gait of, 32
Thong bits, 18, 73, 178
Thorn bits, 97
Thoroughbred, 31; development of, 95–98; as polo pony, 137–141; race tracks for, 118, 120; to stop, 139–141; trainers of, 92, 123
Tie-down, 51, 137, 138
Tigris-Euphrates Valley, 24, 26
Tom Bass Show Bit, 147, 148–149
Tongue lollers, 115, 120–121, 128
Torture and show ring, 31, 92
Tractors, 44, 158, 159–160
Training of colts, 185–194; with hackamore, 164, 188, 192; for harness bits, 102–103; by Indians, 179–180; by whipping, 90, 92
Trotter, 101–102; and racing, 5–6, 123–124
Tutankhamen, 45

Underhill, Francis T., 102, 108–111
United States Cavalry, 169–171, 178; and polo, 134–135

Vices, biting, 162; pulling, 63, 128–129; of race horses, 128–129; 131–132; and severe bits, 197–198

Walking Horses, *see* Tennessee Walking Horses

MELVIN POWERS SELF-IMPROVEMENT LIBRARY

ASTROLOGY

____ ASTROLOGY: HOW TO CHART YOUR HOROSCOPE *Max Heindel*	5.00
____ ASTROLOGY AND SEXUAL ANALYSIS *Morris C. Goodman*	5.00
____ ASTROLOGY AND YOU *Carroll Righter*	5.00
____ ASTROLOGY MADE EASY *Astarte*	5.00
____ ASTROLOGY, ROMANCE, YOU AND THE STARS *Anthony Norvell*	5.00
____ MY WORLD OF ASTROLOGY *Sydney Omarr*	7.00
____ THOUGHT DIAL *Sydney Omarr*	7.00
____ WHAT THE STARS REVEAL ABOUT THE MEN IN YOUR LIFE *Thelma White*	3.00

BRIDGE

____ BRIDGE BIDDING MADE EASY *Edwin B. Kantar*	10.00
____ BRIDGE CONVENTIONS *Edwin B. Kantar*	7.00
____ COMPETITIVE BIDDING IN MODERN BRIDGE *Edgar Kaplan*	7.00
____ DEFENSIVE BRIDGE PLAY COMPLETE *Edwin B. Kantar*	15.00
____ GAMESMAN BRIDGE—PLAY BETTER WITH KANTAR *Edwin B. Kantar*	5.00
____ HOW TO IMPROVE YOUR BRIDGE *Alfred Sheinwold*	5.00
____ IMPROVING YOUR BIDDING SKILLS *Edwin B. Kantar*	4.00
____ INTRODUCTION TO DECLARER'S PLAY *Edwin B. Kantar*	7.00
____ INTRODUCTION TO DEFENDER'S PLAY *Edwin B. Kantar*	7.00
____ KANTAR FOR THE DEFENSE *Edwin B. Kantar*	7.00
____ KANTAR FOR THE DEFENSE VOLUME 2 *Edwin B. Kantar*	7.00
____ TEST YOUR BRIDGE PLAY *Edwin B. Kantar*	5.00
____ VOLUME 2—TEST YOUR BRIDGE PLAY *Edwin B. Kantar*	7.00
____ WINNING DECLARER PLAY *Dorothy Hayden Truscott*	7.00

BUSINESS, STUDY & REFERENCE

____ BRAINSTORMING *Charles Clark*	7.00
____ CONVERSATION MADE EASY *Elliot Russell*	4.00
____ EXAM SECRET *Dennis B. Jackson*	3.00
____ FIX-IT BOOK *Arthur Symons*	2.00
____ HOW TO DEVELOP A BETTER SPEAKING VOICE *M. Hellier*	4.00
____ HOW TO SELF-PUBLISH YOUR BOOK & MAKE IT A BEST SELLER *Melvin Powers*	10.00
____ INCREASE YOUR LEARNING POWER *Geoffrey A. Dudley*	3.00
____ PRACTICAL GUIDE TO BETTER CONCENTRATION *Melvin Powers*	3.00
____ PRACTICAL GUIDE TO PUBLIC SPEAKING *Maurice Forley*	5.00
____ 7 DAYS TO FASTER READING *William S. Schaill*	5.00
____ SONGWRITERS' RHYMING DICTIONARY *Jane Shaw Whitfield*	7.00
____ SPELLING MADE EASY *Lester D. Basch & Dr. Milton Finkelstein*	3.00
____ STUDENT'S GUIDE TO BETTER GRADES *J. A. Rickard*	3.00
____ TEST YOURSELF—FIND YOUR HIDDEN TALENT *Jack Shafer*	3.00
____ YOUR WILL & WHAT TO DO ABOUT IT *Attorney Samuel G. Kling*	5.00

CALLIGRAPHY

____ ADVANCED CALLIGRAPHY *Katherine Jeffares*	7.00
____ CALLIGRAPHER'S REFERENCE BOOK *Anne Leptich & Jacque Evans*	7.00
____ CALLIGRAPHY—THE ART OF BEAUTIFUL WRITING *Katherine Jeffares*	7.00
____ CALLIGRAPHY FOR FUN & PROFIT *Anne Leptich & Jacque Evans*	7.00
____ CALLIGRAPHY MADE EASY *Tina Serafini*	7.00

CHESS & CHECKERS

____ BEGINNER'S GUIDE TO WINNING CHESS *Fred Reinfeld*	5.00
____ CHESS IN TEN EASY LESSONS *Larry Evans*	5.00
____ CHESS MADE EASY *Milton L. Hanauer*	5.00
____ CHESS PROBLEMS FOR BEGINNERS *Edited by Fred Reinfeld*	5.00
____ CHESS TACTICS FOR BEGINNERS *Edited by Fred Reinfeld*	5.00
____ CHESS THEORY & PRACTICE *Morry & Mitchell*	2.00
____ HOW TO WIN AT CHECKERS *Fred Reinfeld*	5.00

_____ 1001 BRILLIANT WAYS TO CHECKMATE *Fred Reinfeld* 7.00
_____ 1001 WINNING CHESS SACRIFICES & COMBINATIONS *Fred Reinfeld* 7.00

COOKERY & HERBS

_____ CULPEPER'S HERBAL REMEDIES *Dr. Nicholas Culpeper* 3.00
_____ FAST GOURMET COOKBOOK *Poppy Cannon* 2.50
_____ GINSENG—THE MYTH & THE TRUTH *Joseph P. Hou* 3.00
_____ HEALING POWER OF HERBS *May Bethel* 5.00
_____ HEALING POWER OF NATURAL FOODS *May Bethel* 5.00
_____ HERBS FOR HEALTH—HOW TO GROW & USE THEM *Louise Evans Doole* 4.00
_____ HOME GARDEN COOKBOOK—DELICIOUS NATURAL FOOD RECIPES *Ken Kraft* 3.00
_____ MEDICAL HERBALIST *Edited by Dr. J. R. Yemm* 3.00
_____ VEGETABLE GARDENING FOR BEGINNERS *Hugh Wiberg* 2.00
_____ VEGETABLES FOR TODAY'S GARDENS *R. Milton Carleton* 2.00
_____ VEGETARIAN COOKERY *Janet Walker* 7.00
_____ VEGETARIAN COOKING MADE EASY & DELECTABLE *Veronica Vezza* 3.00
_____ VEGETARIAN DELIGHTS—A HAPPY COOKBOOK FOR HEALTH *K. R. Mehta* 2.00
_____ VEGETARIAN GOURMET COOKBOOK *Joyce McKinnel* 3.00

GAMBLING & POKER

_____ ADVANCED POKER STRATEGY & WINNING PLAY *A. D. Livingston* 5.00
_____ HOW TO WIN AT DICE GAMES *Skip Frey* 3.00
_____ HOW TO WIN AT POKER *Terence Reese & Anthony T. Watkins* 5.00
_____ WINNING AT CRAPS *Dr. Lloyd T. Commins* 5.00
_____ WINNING AT GIN *Chester Wander & Cy Rice* 3.00
_____ WINNING AT POKER—AN EXPERT'S GUIDE *John Archer* 5.00
_____ WINNING AT 21—AN EXPERT'S GUIDE *John Archer* 5.00
_____ WINNING POKER SYSTEMS *Norman Zadeh* 3.00

HEALTH

_____ BEE POLLEN *Lynda Lyngheim & Jack Scagnetti* 3.00
_____ COPING WITH ALZHEIMER'S *Rose Oliver, Ph.D. & Francis Bock, Ph.D.* 7.00
_____ DR. LINDNER'S SPECIAL WEIGHT CONTROL METHOD *Peter G. Lindner, M.D.* 2.00
_____ HELP YOURSELF TO BETTER SIGHT *Margaret Darst Corbett* 3.00
_____ HOW YOU CAN STOP SMOKING PERMANENTLY *Ernest Caldwell* 5.00
_____ MIND OVER PLATTER *Peter G. Lindner, M.D.* 3.00
_____ NATURE'S WAY TO NUTRITION & VIBRANT HEALTH *Robert J. Scrutton* 3.00
_____ NEW CARBOHYDRATE DIET COUNTER *Patti Lopez-Pereira* 2.00
_____ REFLEXOLOGY *Dr. Maybelle Segal* 4.00
_____ REFLEXOLOGY FOR GOOD HEALTH *Anna Kaye & Don C. Matchan* 5.00
_____ 30 DAYS TO BEAUTIFUL LEGS *Dr. Marc Selner* 3.00
_____ YOU CAN LEARN TO RELAX *Dr. Samuel Gutwirth* 3.00

HOBBIES

_____ BEACHCOMBING FOR BEGINNERS *Norman Hickin* 2.00
_____ BLACKSTONE'S MODERN CARD TRICKS *Harry Blackstone* 5.00
_____ BLACKSTONE'S SECRETS OF MAGIC *Harry Blackstone* 5.00
_____ COIN COLLECTING FOR BEGINNERS *Burton Hobson & Fred Reinfeld* 5.00
_____ ENTERTAINING WITH ESP *Tony 'Doc' Shiels* 2.00
_____ 400 FASCINATING MAGIC TRICKS YOU CAN DO *Howard Thurston* 5.00
_____ HOW I TURN JUNK INTO FUN AND PROFIT *Sari* 3.00
_____ HOW TO WRITE A HIT SONG & SELL IT *Tommy Boyce* 7.00
_____ JUGGLING MADE EASY *Rudolf Dittrich* 3.00
_____ MAGIC FOR ALL AGES *Walter Gibson* 4.00
_____ MAGIC MADE EASY *Byron Wels* 2.00
_____ STAMP COLLECTING FOR BEGINNERS *Burton Hobson* 3.00

HORSE PLAYER'S WINNING GUIDES

_____ BETTING HORSES TO WIN *Les Conklin* 5.00
_____ ELIMINATE THE LOSERS *Bob McKnight* 5.00
_____ HOW TO PICK WINNING HORSES *Bob McKnight* 5.00
_____ HOW TO WIN AT THE RACES *Sam (The Genius) Lewin* 5.00

____ HOW YOU CAN BEAT THE RACES *Jack Kavanagh*		5.00
____ MAKING MONEY AT THE RACES *David Barr*		5.00
____ PAYDAY AT THE RACES *Les Conklin*		5.00
____ SMART HANDICAPPING MADE EASY *William Bauman*		5.00
____ SUCCESS AT THE HARNESS RACES *Barry Meadow*		5.00
____ WINNING AT THE HARNESS RACES—AN EXPERT'S GUIDE *Nick Cammarano*		5.00

HUMOR

____ HOW TO FLATTEN YOUR TUSH *Coach Marge Reardon*		2.00
____ HOW TO MAKE LOVE TO YOURSELF *Ron Stevens & Joy Grdnic*		3.00
____ JOKE TELLER'S HANDBOOK *Bob Orben*		7.00
____ JOKES FOR ALL OCCASIONS *Al Schock*		5.00
____ 2,000 NEW LAUGHS FOR SPEAKERS *Bob Orben*		5.00
____ 2,500 JOKES TO START 'EM LAUGHING *Bob Orben*		7.00

HYPNOTISM

____ ADVANCED TECHNIQUES OF HYPNOSIS *Melvin Powers*		3.00
____ CHILDBIRTH WITH HYPNOSIS *William S. Kroger, M.D.*		5.00
____ HOW TO SOLVE YOUR SEX PROBLEMS WITH SELF-HYPNOSIS *Frank S. Caprio, M.D.*		5.00
____ HOW TO STOP SMOKING THRU SELF-HYPNOSIS *Leslie M. LeCron*		3.00
____ HOW TO USE AUTO-SUGGESTION EFFECTIVELY *John Duckworth*		3.00
____ HOW YOU CAN BOWL BETTER USING SELF-HYPNOSIS *Jack Heise*		4.00
____ HOW YOU CAN PLAY BETTER GOLF USING SELF-HYPNOSIS *Jack Heise*		3.00
____ HYPNOSIS AND SELF-HYPNOSIS *Bernard Hollander, M.D.*		5.00
____ HYPNOTISM *(Originally published in 1893) Carl Sextus*		5.00
____ HYPNOTISM & PSYCHIC PHENOMENA *Simeon Edmunds*		4.00
____ HYPNOTISM MADE EASY *Dr. Ralph Winn*		5.00
____ HYPNOTISM MADE PRACTICAL *Louis Orton*		5.00
____ HYPNOTISM REVEALED *Melvin Powers*		3.00
____ HYPNOTISM TODAY *Leslie LeCron and Jean Bordeaux, Ph.D.*		5.00
____ MODERN HYPNOSIS *Lesley Kuhn & Salvatore Russo, Ph.D.*		5.00
____ NEW CONCEPTS OF HYPNOSIS *Bernard C. Gindes, M.D.*		7.00
____ NEW SELF-HYPNOSIS *Paul Adams*		7.00
____ POST-HYPNOTIC INSTRUCTIONS—SUGGESTIONS FOR THERAPY *Arnold Furst*		5.00
____ PRACTICAL GUIDE TO SELF-HYPNOSIS *Melvin Powers*		3.00
____ PRACTICAL HYPNOTISM *Philip Magonet, M.D.*		3.00
____ SECRETS OF HYPNOTISM *S. J. Van Pelt, M.D.*		5.00
____ SELF-HYPNOSIS—A CONDITIONED-RESPONSE TECHNIQUE *Laurence Sparks*		7.00
____ SELF-HYPNOSIS—ITS THEORY, TECHNIQUE & APPLICATION *Melvin Powers*		3.00
____ THERAPY THROUGH HYPNOSIS *Edited by Raphael H. Rhodes*		5.00

JUDAICA

____ SERVICE OF THE HEART *Evelyn Garfiel, Ph.D.*		7.00
____ STORY OF ISRAEL IN COINS *Jean & Maurice Gould*		2.00
____ STORY OF ISRAEL IN STAMPS *Maxim & Gabriel Shamir*		1.00
____ TONGUE OF THE PROPHETS *Robert St. John*		7.00

JUST FOR WOMEN

____ COSMOPOLITAN'S GUIDE TO MARVELOUS MEN Foreword by *Helen Gurley Brown*		3.00
____ COSMOPOLITAN'S HANG-UP HANDBOOK Foreword by *Helen Gurley Brown*		4.00
____ COSMOPOLITAN'S LOVE BOOK—A GUIDE TO ECSTASY IN BED		7.00
____ COSMOPOLITAN'S NEW ETIQUETTE GUIDE Foreword by *Helen Gurley Brown*		4.00
____ I AM A COMPLEAT WOMAN *Doris Hagopian & Karen O'Connor Sweeney*		3.00
____ JUST FOR WOMEN—A GUIDE TO THE FEMALE BODY *Richard E. Sand, M.D.*		5.00
____ NEW APPROACHES TO SEX IN MARRIAGE *John E. Eichenlaub, M.D.*		3.00
____ SEXUALLY ADEQUATE FEMALE *Frank S. Caprio, M.D.*		3.00
____ SEXUALLY FULFILLED WOMAN *Dr. Rachel Copelan*		5.00
____ YOUR FIRST YEAR OF MARRIAGE *Dr. Tom McGinnis*		3.00

MARRIAGE, SEX & PARENTHOOD

____ ABILITY TO LOVE *Dr. Allan Fromme*		7.00
____ GUIDE TO SUCCESSFUL MARRIAGE *Drs. Albert Ellis & Robert Harper*		7.00

____ HOW TO RAISE AN EMOTIONALLY HEALTHY, HAPPY CHILD *Albert Ellis, Ph.D.*   7.00
____ PARENT SURVIVAL TRAINING *Marvin Silverman, Ed.D. & David Lustig, Ph.D.*   10.00
____ SEX WITHOUT GUILT *Albert Ellis, Ph.D.*   5.00
____ SEXUALLY ADEQUATE MALE *Frank S. Caprio, M.D.*   3.00
____ SEXUALLY FULFILLED MAN *Dr. Rachel Copelan*   5.00
____ STAYING IN LOVE *Dr. Norton F. Kristy*   7.00

MELVIN POWERS' MAIL ORDER LIBRARY

____ HOW TO GET RICH IN MAIL ORDER *Melvin Powers*   20.00
____ HOW TO WRITE A GOOD ADVERTISEMENT *Victor O. Schwab*   20.00
____ MAIL ORDER MADE EASY *J. Frank Brumbaugh*   20.00

METAPHYSICS & OCCULT

____ BOOK OF TALISMANS, AMULETS & ZODIACAL GEMS *William Pavitt*   7.00
____ CONCENTRATION—A GUIDE TO MENTAL MASTERY *Mouni Sadhu*   5.00
____ EXTRA-TERRESTRIAL INTELLIGENCE—THE FIRST ENCOUNTER   6.00
____ FORTUNE TELLING WITH CARDS *P. Foli*   5.00
____ HOW TO INTERPRET DREAMS, OMENS & FORTUNE TELLING SIGNS *Gettings*   5.00
____ HOW TO UNDERSTAND YOUR DREAMS *Geoffrey A. Dudley*   5.00
____ IN DAYS OF GREAT PEACE *Mouni Sadhu*   3.00
____ LSD—THE AGE OF MIND *Bernard Roseman*   2.00
____ MAGICIAN—HIS TRAINING AND WORK *W. E. Butler*   5.00
____ MEDITATION *Mouni Sadhu*   7.00
____ MODERN NUMEROLOGY *Morris C. Goodman*   5.00
____ NUMEROLOGY—ITS FACTS AND SECRETS *Ariel Yvon Taylor*   5.00
____ NUMEROLOGY MADE EASY *W. Mykian*   5.00
____ PALMISTRY MADE EASY *Fred Gettings*   5.00
____ PALMISTRY MADE PRACTICAL *Elizabeth Daniels Squire*   5.00
____ PALMISTRY SECRETS REVEALED *Henry Frith*   4.00
____ PROPHECY IN OUR TIME *Martin Ebon*   2.50
____ SUPERSTITION—ARE YOU SUPERSTITIOUS? *Eric Maple*   2.00
____ TAROT *Mouni Sadhu*   10.00
____ TAROT OF THE BOHEMIANS *Papus*   7.00
____ WAYS TO SELF-REALIZATION *Mouni Sadhu*   7.00
____ WITCHCRAFT, MAGIC & OCCULTISM—A FASCINATING HISTORY *W. B. Crow*   7.00
____ WITCHCRAFT—THE SIXTH SENSE *Justine Glass*   7.00
____ WORLD OF PSYCHIC RESEARCH *Hereward Carrington*   2.00

SELF-HELP & INSPIRATIONAL

____ CHARISMA—HOW TO GET "THAT SPECIAL MAGIC" *Marcia Grad*   7.00
____ DAILY POWER FOR JOYFUL LIVING *Dr. Donald Curtis*   5.00
____ DYNAMIC THINKING *Melvin Powers*   5.00
____ GREATEST POWER IN THE UNIVERSE *U. S. Andersen*   7.00
____ GROW RICH WHILE YOU SLEEP *Ben Sweetland*   7.00
____ GROWTH THROUGH REASON *Albert Ellis, Ph.D.*   7.00
____ GUIDE TO PERSONAL HAPPINESS *Albert Ellis, Ph.D. & Irving Becker, Ed.D.*   7.00
____ HANDWRITING ANALYSIS MADE EASY *John Marley*   5.00
____ HANDWRITING TELLS *Nadya Olyanova*   7.00
____ HOW TO ATTRACT GOOD LUCK *A.H.Z. Carr*   7.00
____ HOW TO BE GREAT *Dr. Donald Curtis*   5.00
____ HOW TO DEVELOP A WINNING PERSONALITY *Martin Panzer*   5.00
____ HOW TO DEVELOP AN EXCEPTIONAL MEMORY *Young & Gibson*   5.00
____ HOW TO LIVE WITH A NEUROTIC *Albert Ellis, Ph.D.*   7.00
____ HOW TO OVERCOME YOUR FEARS *M. P. Leahy, M.D.*   3.00
____ HOW TO SUCCEED *Brian Adams*   7.00
____ HUMAN PROBLEMS & HOW TO SOLVE THEM *Dr. Donald Curtis*   5.00
____ I CAN *Ben Sweetland*   7.00
____ I WILL *Ben Sweetland*   3.00
____ KNIGHT IN THE RUSTY ARMOR *Robert Fisher*   5.00
____ LEFT-HANDED PEOPLE *Michael Barsley*   5.00

_____ MAGIC IN YOUR MIND *U.S. Andersen*	7.00
_____ MAGIC OF THINKING BIG *Dr. David J. Schwartz*	3.00
_____ MAGIC OF THINKING SUCCESS *Dr. David J. Schwartz*	7.00
_____ MAGIC POWER OF YOUR MIND *Walter M. Germain*	7.00
_____ MENTAL POWER THROUGH SLEEP SUGGESTION *Melvin Powers*	3.00
_____ NEVER UNDERESTIMATE THE SELLING POWER OF A WOMAN *Dottie Walters*	7.00
_____ NEW GUIDE TO RATIONAL LIVING *Albert Ellis, Ph.D. & R. Harper, Ph.D.*	7.00
_____ PSYCHO-CYBERNETICS *Maxwell Maltz, M.D.*	7.00
_____ PSYCHOLOGY OF HANDWRITING *Nadya Olyanova*	7.00
_____ SALES CYBERNETICS *Brian Adams*	7.00
_____ SCIENCE OF MIND IN DAILY LIVING *Dr. Donald Curtis*	7.00
_____ SECRET OF SECRETS *U.S. Andersen*	7.00
_____ SECRET POWER OF THE PYRAMIDS *U. S. Andersen*	7.00
_____ SELF-THERAPY FOR THE STUTTERER *Malcolm Frazer*	3.00
_____ SUCCESS-CYBERNETICS *U. S. Andersen*	7.00
_____ 10 DAYS TO A GREAT NEW LIFE *William E. Edwards*	3.00
_____ THINK AND GROW RICH *Napoleon Hill*	7.00
_____ THREE MAGIC WORDS *U. S. Andersen*	7.00
_____ TREASURY OF COMFORT *Edited by Rabbi Sidney Greenberg*	7.00
_____ TREASURY OF THE ART OF LIVING *Sidney S. Greenberg*	7.00
_____ WHAT YOUR HANDWRITING REVEALS *Albert E. Hughes*	3.00
_____ YOUR SUBCONSCIOUS POWER *Charles M. Simmons*	7.00
_____ YOUR THOUGHTS CAN CHANGE YOUR LIFE *Dr. Donald Curtis*	7.00

SPORTS

_____ BICYCLING FOR FUN AND GOOD HEALTH *Kenneth E. Luther*	2.00
_____ BILLIARDS—POCKET • CAROM • THREE CUSION *Clive Cottingham, Jr.*	5.00
_____ COMPLETE GUIDE TO FISHING *Vlad Evanoff*	2.00
_____ HOW TO IMPROVE YOUR RACQUETBALL *Lubarsky, Kaufman & Scagnetti*	5.00
_____ HOW TO WIN AT POCKET BILLIARDS *Edward D. Knuchell*	7.00
_____ JOY OF WALKING *Jack Scagnetti*	3.00
_____ LEARNING & TEACHING SOCCER SKILLS *Eric Worthington*	3.00
_____ MOTORCYCLING FOR BEGINNERS *I.G. Edmonds*	3.00
_____ RACQUETBALL FOR WOMEN *Toni Hudson, Jack Scagnetti & Vince Rondone*	3.00
_____ RACQUETBALL MADE EASY *Steve Lubarsky, Rod Delson & Jack Scagnetti*	5.00
_____ SECRET OF BOWLING STRIKES *Dawson Taylor*	5.00
_____ SECRET OF PERFECT PUTTING *Horton Smith & Dawson Taylor*	5.00
_____ SOCCER—THE GAME & HOW TO PLAY IT *Gary Rosenthal*	5.00
_____ STARTING SOCCER *Edward F. Dolan, Jr.*	5.00

TENNIS LOVER'S LIBRARY

_____ BEGINNER'S GUIDE TO WINNING TENNIS *Helen Hull Jacobs*	2.00
_____ HOW TO BEAT BETTER TENNIS PLAYERS *Loring Fiske*	4.00
_____ HOW TO IMPROVE YOUR TENNIS—STYLE, STRATEGY & ANALYSIS *C. Wilson*	2.00
_____ PSYCH YOURSELF TO BETTER TENNIS *Dr. Walter A. Luszki*	2.00
_____ TENNIS FOR BEGINNERS *Dr. H. A. Murray*	2.00
_____ TENNIS MADE EASY *Joel Brecheen*	5.00
_____ WEEKEND TENNIS—HOW TO HAVE FUN & WIN AT THE SAME TIME *Bill Talbert*	3.00
_____ WINNING WITH PERCENTAGE TENNIS—SMART STRATEGY *Jack Lowe*	2.00

WILSHIRE PET LIBRARY

_____ DOG OBEDIENCE TRAINING *Gust Kessopulos*	5.00
_____ DOG TRAINING MADE EASY & FUN *John W. Kellogg*	5.00
_____ HOW TO BRING UP YOUR PET DOG *Kurt Unkelbach*	2.00
_____ HOW TO RAISE & TRAIN YOUR PUPPY *Jeff Griffen*	5.00

The books listed above can be obtained from your book dealer or directly from Melvin Powers. When ordering, please remit $1.50 postage for the first book and 50¢ for each additional book.

Melvin Powers
12015 Sherman Road, No. Hollywood, California 91605